A Light Reflected

by

Dr. Mary C. McDonald

ISBN: 1-4140-7522-7 (e-book)
ISBN: 1-4140-7521-9 (Paperback)

Library of Congress Control Number: 2004091010

This book is printed on acid free paper.

Printed in the United States of America
Bloomington, IN

1st Books - rev. 03/16/04

DEDICATION

To God, with whom all things are possible

~

To my husband, Joe, whose love is one of the miracles in my life.

~

To my parents, Mary and Joe Crowley, who grounded me in a life well-lived by their love and example.

~

To my children, Matthew and Christine, who taught me how to be a parent, and how to see with my heart.

~

To my Son-in-Law, Scott, and Daughter-in-Law, Kate, who broadened my circle of love and friendship.

~

To my grandchildren, Nick, Emma, Molly, Elise, Jack and Annie, who gift me with wonder and miracles, and light.

~

Contents

Section One:
A Light Reflected In A Parent's Heart

Section Two:
A Light Reflected In A Life Well-lived

Section Three:
A Light Reflected In A Journey Home

ACKNOWLEDGEMENTS

A MIRACLE FOR ALL SEASONS

I know a miracle when I see one. I recognize the signs. There is always a light that reveals the invisible, a fiat that gives form to the intangible, and a courageous redemption of hope. The interesting thing about miracles is that they often come disguised and humble, like the rock that changes the course of a river. God authors them and they never come alone.

Before Bishop J. Terry Steib, S.V.D. came to Memphis, before I was Superintendent of Schools, I heard him speak at a meeting in New Orleans. He said that although Catholic education was declining in the inner cities, it was not dead. He said that it was up to us, the educators, to bring it back to life. He challenged us that Easter week to, "Roll back the stone!" God sowed the seeds of hope that day, everywhere. God sowed them in the hearts of all those who longed to reclaim the hope of children born into hopelessness. Little did I know, as I sat there, inspired by Bishop Steib's words, that he would come to Memphis to roll back that stone, and that I would get to help push.

There is a persistent divide in our society between those who have plenty and those who suffer poverty. That ever-widening gap threatens our collective freedom. Catholic education in this country was founded to address the needs of children in poverty, children of immigrant populations, children without choices. That was the vision that Bishop Steib brought with him to Memphis. A vision that bridged the divide of poverty with hope, the divide of ignorance with education. He caused us to remember that it is our heritage to educate those who need us most.

When Bishop Steib appointed me Superintendent, he shared this vision with me. I knew what he was asking would take a miracle. How would we address this great need? We worked and we prayed. And God heard our prayers and blessed our efforts. The seeds of hope He planted in others' hearts who also sought to help children in poverty, bloomed and bore fruit that led them to us. These generous Good Samaritans' donation was the seed that allowed us to begin to reclaim our mission of education in the poverty areas of Memphis and begin the miracle of our Catholic Urban initiative, our Jubilee Schools. These Donors, like the Wise Men, longed only to see hope in the face of a child. The reopening of the seven long-closed inner city Catholic schools began in July of 1999. All seven school are reopened now, and serving the children and families in the most underserved areas of Memphis.

And God's seeds continue to bloom in the hearts of those whom He calls to serve in these Jubilee Schools, those who support the work of these schools with their gifts of time, talent, treasure and prayer and those who continue to seek ways to ensure that these schools will continue.

I know that the Jubilee Schools are a miracle; all the signs are there. They witness to God's greatness; His providence bridges the divide of poverty with hope, the divide of ignorance with education for all God's children.

I am deeply grateful to Bishop Steib, a man of great faith, for giving me the opportunity to be part of a miracle and to serve the children who need us most.

~

A portion of the proceeds from the sale of this book will be donated to the Catholic Memphis Urban Schools and Jubilee Schools Scholarship Funds

INTRODUCTION

And God said, "Let there be light".
Genesis, Chapter one

Several years ago, my family and I drove from Memphis, Tennessee to El Paso, Texas. It would have been much faster to fly, but I am glad we drove. If we had taken a plane, I would have missed the experience of driving across a dessert at night. I don't think I ever really noticed before just how ominous the dark can be. It didn't take long to loose perspective of what was around us. The headlights on the car revealed only the sameness of the immediate flat road ahead. We drove, not guided by the lights of the car, but by the light of faith. It was faith that the road we were on would take us to our destination. There were more than a few times that I sensed being lost but there was nothing to do but to continue on the road. Then we saw it. The lights of El Paso reflected in the night sky. Everything would be fine now. We saw the light.

There are times when all of us, as we journey through life, learn just how ominous the dark can be. We learn just how difficult staying on the right path can be. We learn how to trust when we cannot see what is ahead. We learn how to see with eyes of faith. We learn to see the light, reflected. And when we learn, we teach.

A Light Reflected is a collection of lessons learned and taught. We are all teachers. We are all students. We learn from one another. We see into the life of things when we sense the interconnectedness of what happens as we journey through life. It is the light by which we travel that makes all the difference as to where we go, and how we get there. That light is reflected in the choices we make, the life we lead, what we teach, and from whom we learn.

For me, there is only one light. "For God who said, 'Let light shine out of darkness', made His light shine on our hearts to give the light of knowledge of the Glory of God in the face of Christ." (2 Cor 4:6). So, I seek His face, His light. It is this light that is reflected in the hearts and lives and faces of everyone I see. And they all teach me. So I learn. So I teach.

SECTION ONE:

A LIGHT REFLECTED

IN

A PARENT'S HEART

A Parents' Pledge

We are people of ceremony and ritual. Every occasion of transition is cause for celebration. A prescribed formula marks our rite of passage from one status to another. Significant milestones are pronounced by traditional words stating our readiness to take on the new responsibility. Marriage, Baptism, Confirmation, membership initiations, oaths of office, and graduations, all are marked by ritual. All the new responsibilities are accounted for, all but the most significant, parenthood. A hospital bill is usually the only thing presented to new parents. Becoming a parent needs a ritual. If your parenthood has not been "ritualized" yet, may I suggest the following ritual?

By the authority vested in me by God, I am pronounced a parent.
I give up the right to remain silent. Anything I neglect to say or do that will help my child to become a better person, can and will be held against me in the court of heaven.
I have the right to say, "I love you".
I have the right to say "no".
I have the right to exercise my judgment as a parent free from the pressures of my peers and society.
I have the right to openly struggle to live in faith within the circumstances of our unique family life.
I have the right to freely give my child acceptance for who he/she is, not what he/she is.

I have the right to simplify our family life by deciding realistically what we want to do and what we have time to do.

I have the right to put God in the center of my life and the life of my family.

I have the responsibility to speak out against the evil that diminishes the value of all life.

I have the responsibility to provide my child with the lasting gifts of positive role models, beginning with myself.

I will use my God-given parental instincts to guide me in the choices I make for my child. Before each decision, I will weigh the consequences and seek to bring out the best in all involved.

I will respect my child's other parent.

I relinquish the right to reach back through the mist of my past to relive in my child what was never lived in me.

I relinquish my rigid attachment to a specific outcome and will live in the wisdom of uncertainty.

I will relinquish my authority as a parent only to my child, and only after he/she proves his/her ability to accept the responsibilities of a mature adult.

I am guided by love, supported by prayer, strengthened by faith, and encouraged by God's trust in me, a parent.

Having declared this, I will go forth and parent, so help me, God.

Try it. It could be a ritual that works.

~

Parenting, A Gift Of Love

One evening, while sorting out my decorations for the approaching holiday season, my entire life flashed before my eyes. It was not a near-death experience that caused this to happen, but a quick glance around that black hole I call an attic. In cartons and on racks and on nails in the wall were countless treasures waiting for future generations to throw out. I guess I'll die before I move and because I'll never live long enough to pack it all. One box, amid the stacks of boxes, did manage to catch my eye. It was a box of "How To" books on raising children.

As I leafed through the books, I realized how much of the advice contained in them I didn't take, mostly because I was too busy raising my children to remember what I read. There is one book, however, I have used as a constant source of wisdom. That one is not in the attic, but rather, next to my bed.

Whenever parenting seemed a little too difficult and I would grow weary of the struggles, I would meditate on Corinthians Chapter 13 and mentally substitute the word parenting for the word love. It would go something like this:

Parenting is the gift of Love. Now I will show you the way, which surpasses all the others.
Parenting is patient, even with babies who cry all night or children who want drinks of water or hear

"noises" all night or adolescents who want to stay out all night.

Parenting is kind; it appreciates the efforts of homemade surprises that leave messy kitchens and the beauty in a haircut that didn't quite work out.

Parenting is not jealous - of other children's accomplishments and other parents' success.

Parenting is never rude, it respects and cherishes.

Parenting is not prone to anger but to the strength to hold firm to the values of the family.

Parenting does not rejoice in what is wrong but rejoices in the truth.

There is joy in doing what is right even if you're the only one doing it.

There is no limit to a parent's forbearance, to a parent's trust in God, to a parent's hope and a parent's ability to endure.

There are, in the end, after all of the books about parenting I have read, only three strategies that have lasted: faith, hope and love. And they are all in the same book, the Bible.

~

Honor Thy Father And Thy Mother

What ever happened to the Commandment that says, "Honor thy father and thy mother"? It used to be one of the big ones. It was talked about in churches and schools and reinforced at home. We knew the status of parenthood and parents. When God said, "Honor thy father and mother" He vested in parents the authority to instruct, direct, lead and mentor His children back to Him.

Right after establishing His importance in our lives in the first three Commandments, God emphasizes the importance of parents in the lives of their children. He bestows upon parents the authority and courage to make the decisions necessary to guide their children on the path of moral maturity. He established the criteria for success. Successful parenting is based on the fundamental truth that God exists and that we, as parents, are responsible to Him for the children He has given us. When God said, "Honor thy Father and Mother," He let the kids know who's in charge. It is up to us to firmly establish that authority in our minds and in the minds of our children.

Our parenting is shaped by our faith. It is sustained by holding on to that faith and creating the moral environment in our families in which parenting our children will take place. Parents are the first teachers of their children. The lessons our children learn from us are the cornerstones of their spiritual, social, emotional, psychological and moral development.

Before we can teach our children, we need to be sure that we have laid a firm foundation of our own; so that we will have the strength and resources we need when all that we know and believe is challenged.

In the past few years, our society has rewritten the Commandments to suit the changing times. Parents are often held hostage by a culture that tells them the importance of parents honoring their children to the point of compromising their own standards. The world in which we live looks at results. We are obsessed with outcomes that are based on a secular standard as a measure of our parenting. The world cannot reproduce real parenting when the world, in spite of material prosperity, is suffering from spiritual poverty. Real parenting is concerned about eternal rewards and practiced by parents who know that no worldly success is the measure of a child's true worth. When trying to establish family values, parents often fall victim to peer and societal pressure that says good parenting is giving your child everything he/she wants. God says good parenting is giving your child everything he/she needs. God does no less for us. Why would we want to do less for our children?

Often, in our zeal to provide a perfect world for our children, we deny them the opportunity for growth and character development. As parents, we teach with our actions and our lives. If we give our children everything and never say "no", our children will expect no less of the world. Our zeal should be directed toward instilling in our children the moral courage it

takes to meet the challenges of life and to stand by his/
her principles no matter how difficult. An appropriate
"no" is often more loving than a million inappropriate
"yeses."

God has given us the permission and with authority to
parent, by allowing His own Son to be subject to the
parenting of Mary and Joseph. God allowed them to
trust their instincts and to do what was best for His
Son. If "honoring thy Father and Mother" was good
enough for God's child to follow, then it's good enough
for our children to follow, too. Commit to living this
Commandment, now. Commit to being a parent who
will not flinch in face of worldly standards but lives in
the light of God's truth.

~

Just Like A Mother

There is a church in Rome, a city of churches that is truly unique in the entire world. It is the oldest church in Rome dedicated to Mary, the Mother of Jesus. It is not the age, or the architecture, of Santa Maria in Trastervere that makes it so special to me. It is the 750-year old mosaic in the apse behind the main altar. The gold-flecked tiles depict the risen Christ, on His throne of glory, surrounded by St. Peter and by the early Popes who ministered at Santa Maria. Seated at His right hand, on the sane throne, at His side, is His mother, Mary, a gold crown on her head. Christ's arm, in a gesture of gratitude and recognition, is around Mary's shoulders.

It is a familiar pose in a family album. It is the gesture of an adult-to-adult, of close cooperation, of equality, not of their natures, but of their commitment and realized hopes. I have many pictures with my arm resting around my mother's shoulders taken at those milestone events in my life. I have pictures of my children's arms on my shoulders at graduations, weddings and family reunions. The gesture always seems to have the same meaning regardless of the event, "Thanks Mom". I have been in a lot of churches and seen hundreds of pictures of Jesus with His mother. Most depicted an infant, sweet and dependent, nestled in His mother's arms. Some portrayed the agony of a man, dying on a cross while His mother stood watch. Only this one mosaic shows a grown man, acknowledging His mother as a woman of influence and strength. He's thanking her for recognizing that His would be a hard and lonely journey and for understanding His need for her love and support as He carried out His mission of sacrifice and redemption. But then, isn't that just like a mother?

Mary was a woman of insight, patience and strength. She was a mother who was on an assignment from God to teach her son God's Word and wisdom. She was a woman after God's own heart, ready to do His will. Like most mothers, she instinctively knew when to ponder and when to act. When her Son was twelve, she reined in His youthful spirit of adventure. When Her Son was thirty, she gently, but firmly, nudged Him into his mission. When He was thirty-three, she stood, keeping a brave watch by the cross, determined to remain with Him, encouraging Him by her presence. With His dying breath, Jesus acknowledged her witness of faith as an example for us all. But then, isn't that just like a mother?

A mother has the ability to see what lies beyond the present circumstance of her child, no matter how old her child, no matter how long it takes. A mother sees what lies beyond for the newborn, the late-bloomer, and the rebellious teen. A mother sees what lies beyond the indecision and fear of the college-bound, the job seeker, and the one on the brink of a lifetime commitment. A mother keeps a brave watch for her distant child, her addicted child, and her confused child. A mother remains at the side of her dying child, her condemned child, her child in crisis. A mother cradles her child in her love forever and her heart encourages the gifts of her gift to the world. But then, isn't that just like a mother?

It is no coincidence that Jesus' ministry grew out of His family life and His relationship with His mother. It is no coincidence that our own journey does the same. Mary taught us that all things are possible with God. She showed us how to follow the inspirations of grace with a purity of intention. She exemplified a reliance on faith in the face of doubt. She bore misunderstandings, trials and anguish in humble silence. She linked humanity with divinity and made us aware of Christ's presence within us. She loved faithfully and joyfully. But then, isn't that just like a mother?

~

Who's Listening To Noah?

I never thought of Noah as a role model for parents, until recently that is. I was speaking to a group of parents not long ago, listening to their concerns about raising children in such a dangerous world. They felt as if every conversation they had lately with their children was a warning about a very real possibility of some harm coming to them. It was becoming increasingly more difficult to answer their children's questions without adding to their fears. I understood their concerns. Sometimes we see so much evil around us, we almost forget what trust feels like. How do we know who is right, who is wrong? How do we know who is friend, who if foe? Who let in all the wolves in sheep's clothing? As they spoke, I thought, "Society is not paying attention to its prophets". Not the prophets of doom, the prophets of hope. Who is listening to Noah? Who is trusting God?

It is not easy for parents to be a voice that is counter to a popular way of doing things in society. It was not easy for Noah either. He, in spite of ridicule and scorn by others, continued to do what he thought was right for his family. He was faithful to the mission God gave him. It could not have been easy. If you have ever taken a family trip then you know the pitfalls. I can hear it now, "I don't like boats. Why can't we ride one of the beasts?" "Why do I have to go, none of my friends are going?" "Why do the elephants always get to sit next to the window?" "Why do we always have to be different, everyone thinks you're crazy".

"Johnny's Dad said it doesn't even look like rain, and he's real smart". But Noah was faithful to the word of God. That was not an easy task for a man who just invited his entire family and their pets on an extended cruise.

Because of Noah's faithfulness, God gave him an insight into a coming disaster. God also told him what to do to avoid the disaster and how he could save his family. Build an Ark. Whether or not those Noah warned of the impending dangers believed him, he still continued to build. Noah heard God's wake-up call. It's the same call God sends today. It is not a call to doom, but to hope. And that hope lies in listening to God's plan for our families and taking action. God's promise to Noah was fulfilled because Noah stuck to his mission to build an ark, to gather his family together and travel the journey God laid out for them.

Perhaps it's time for us to build an ark, an ark we call "family". Perhaps it's time to draw our families closer to the values we espouse, the virtues we practice and the Faith we believe. Perhaps it's time to shut out some of the influences in the world that only serve to weaken our resolve to raise our children according to our own, God-given spiritual instincts. Perhaps it is time to encourage others by our example and by our invitation to them to share this journey with us, to be family for each other. Perhaps it is time to understand that we are all in God's family. Perhaps we need to learn that we really are all in this boat together, and, for the sake of the children, all God's children, perhaps we should build that ark together. Regardless of what others say or do, perhaps we should just keep building our family according to God's plan. It is there, in that family, that we will keep alive all that is good. And that family will float in the knowledge that no matter what happens, God keeps His promises. Perhaps we should be more like Noah.

~

A Mother's Gifts

Mothers' Day presents are very special gifts. It is not so much for what they are but for the love they convey. I remember when I was a child saving money and looking forward to surprising my mother with the best gift in the world. I was always listening for clues as to what she might like to have. Clues I didn't always pick up on. One year it was a huge box of hairpins. Another year it was blue bottle of Evening in Paris perfume. Once I gave her a really cool coconut, with a hand-carved face on it, teeth and all.

Every year she would open the gifts with such enthusiasm that I was convinced I had given her the crown jewels. Mothers are like that. More often than not, she'd carefully place the gifts in her "Special Drawer". It was a place she kept things to be used only on special occasions. It was a very big deal to have one of your gifts in the "Special Drawer". I am sure that coconut head is still in the drawer, since I don't remember any occasion special enough for her to hang it up. My mother made that ritual as much a part of Mothers' Day as the gifts themselves. Mothers are like that, too. They recognize the giver much more than the gift. Yet, they do not always recognize what a gift they are to others.

I still think Mothers' Day gifts are special. But, over the years, I learned that the greatest Mother's Day gift came from God Himself. Christ, dying on the cross, gave us His own mother as our mentor, our role model, and

our mother. *In that gift, He raised not only mothers,
but also all women, to the place He first intended them
to be. We need to live in that place. We need to be
mothers, grandmothers, women who can teach other
women Christian character. We need to that others are
observing the decisions we make and will learn from
us. As women of faith, we must reclaim the dignity
of women for those who follow us. We must live our
lives with grace and humility and by our example belie
the status we have inherited from a world filled with
deception, immorality, pornography and lies. Our
world needs heroines of character and strength who
are unafraid to unleash the power of love to combat
a culture of violence and death. We need women who
will respect all life and encourage the heart of another.
We need mothers who will give witness to the sign of
God in their lives.*

*For mothers, for all women entrusted with the glorious
mission of encouraging new life through their service
to others, this is the gift Christ gave us when He gave
us the gift of His mother. You don't have to wait to
use it, the special occasion is now. Take your gifts out
of the drawer and use them to encourage, to nurture,
to "mother" new life in the life of another and in our
world.*

~

A Father's Legacy

I know that Mrs. Bruce Dodd started Father's Day in 1909, but I bet it was her father who chose the date. He probably cringed at the thought of receiving another tie and convinced her to pick a summer date in the hopes of making it more of an outdoor, guy thing. When I was growing up, it definitely was. The annual Father's Day bar-b-que was an event fit for a king who had just received the latest in outdoor cooking necessities. I thought my father was the greatest chef in the world when it came to outdoor cooking. Thinking about it now, actually, he was the greatest at delegating.

Before the event, while my mother was preparing all but the meat, my father gave each of my four brothers and me an assignment that was crucial to the outcome of the annual Father's Day celebration. The assignments were rotated each year since two of the jobs were perceived as "more important" than the others. Being his assistant and "manning" the hose were the most prestigious assignments. I liked being my father's assistant and passing him the salt and pepper, holding the fork or running into the house for forgotten items, but "manning" the hose was the best. You could always count on dousing a few blazing hamburgers. Somehow my father convinced us that charred was good. To this day, that's my preference for hot dogs. But the Father's Day bar-b-que was never really about the food cooked or the gifts received. I was really about nourishing family and recognizing the importance of each member, not for what they do, but for who they are. Fathers do that. You don't have to be anything more than his child to be important in the eyes of a father. It's a gift granted by God to all fathers. It's called unconditional love.

Before Jesus began His public ministry, He went to John to be baptized. "After Jesus was baptized, he came up from the water and behold, the heavens were opened and he saw the spirit of God, descending like a dove upon him. And a voice came from the heavens saying, "This is my beloved son in whom I am well pleased"." (Matt: 3,13-14). I used to wonder why God didn't save such public accolades for the Resurrection. Praise for the completion of a job well done is so much more a part of our understanding. Following in your father's footsteps is a highly rewarded part of our culture, no matter what the footsteps are. Laying claim to the bragging rights of saying, "my son/daughter the ____ ___", is much more familiar to us. But Jesus had not accomplished anything yet. Why was there such a display of affection?

I realize now, that in that demonstration of love at Jesus' baptism, God gave to all fathers the example of the unconditional love a father has for his child. You don't have to do anything more important than be his child. You hold the potential of his hopes, but whether fulfilled or not, he is well pleased. We are beloved to God because we are, not because we do. What an awesome father's day gift. It is one that never wears out and can't be replaced. It is a father's inheritance from God the Father. Use it often. Let it be the legacy of all fathers, and all men, to use the God-given gift of unconditional love to nurture the heart of another.

~

When Elephants Fight

There is an African saying that "When elephants fight, only the grass gets trampled". Since my only encounters with elephants, real or otherwise, is limited to an occasional trip to the zoo and countless viewings of Dumbo, I really didn't understand the significance of that saying until I saw elephants fight on an Animal Planet show on TV. It didn't actually look like fighting. It was more like intimidation by sheer weight and size, posturing for the turf they trampled. They were too big to even look down at the damage beneath their feet. The grass was too insignificant to matter. I decided to focus on the grass. It was then that I realized what that saying meant. When the elephants of society fight, it is those who are powerless who get trampled. It is the ones who can't fight back. The ones overpowered by the weight and size of the elephants are never noticed. In our society today, it is the children who get trampled. It is they who bear the weight of the fighting elephants.

The elephants fight and the most powerless of children, the unborn, die. The rulers, the power-brokers, the forces of this darkness of greed and spiritual decay, posture for turf and our children fall victim to the reality of evil. They live the effects of this evil every day as they experience abuse, neglect, loneliness, fear, overindulgence, weakness, poverty, and materialism. The world does not have the best interest of the children at heart, but the best interest of the powers that be. Why would we wonder why there are children who *are violent, addicted to drugs and alcohol, sexually promiscuous, obscene in speech and dress, immoral and amoral in behavior? Why wouldn't there be? Our society has fertilized them with role models, with heroes, with leaders in all fields who are the same. Our children are not safe in their homes; they are unsafe explorers without guides in a cyberspace world of virtual reality. Telling our children to "Just say no" is like telling the grass to get out of the way of a thundering herd of elephants.*

Yet the grass is not dead. Our children's roots lie deep in the heart of a compassionate God.

Childhood has been suspended by a society that is spiritually asleep. Who will resurrect it? Who will roll back the stone? Who will post the sign that says, "Keep Off The Grass"? Who will cooperate with God in the miraculous process of transformation? It is necessary for someone to carry the cross, weather the storm, and stand firm in the face of opposition. Let it be the adults, not the children. Who will protect the children and lead them out of this darkness? If not us, who? If not now, when? Our hope lies in the knowledge that what we seek to conquer has already been vanquished by Christ's death and resurrection.

I know there are many parents who feel alone, discouraged and confused. They feel the weight of a world that seems to celebrate a lack of values and many are chided for the moral stands they take. They are confronted with choices they never planned to make when society confuses tolerance for the sinner with tolerance for the sin. They are pressured to compete and led to believe that their parenting is judged by their child's ability to be the best, to have the most. They don't need blame. They need support. They need compassion.

No matter how strong a parent is, the potential to burn out, to give in, will fade in the light of encouragement and compassion received from those who believe that with God's grace and strengthened by prayer, things can be changed. Parents must reclaim their authority. Parents must "Just say no". Parents must know we care, God cares. Faith is the father of miracles, compassion the mother. Our faith in God's power has been buried behind a stone of fear, uncertainty and doubt. Roll back the stone! Allow the compassion of Christ to give us the strength to stand firm in our convictions, the courage to support each other, and the resolve to keep the elephants off the grass.

~

A Search For Independence

Not long ago, parents, worried and confused about the behavior of their adolescent child, asked for my prayers. I prayed that they would recognize that what they continued to pray for the already received. When we have waited so long and prayed so hard for something, our mind often tricks us into not recognizing our answer when it comes. They wanted their child to resist temptation and change his behavior. What they needed was to recognize their authority and strength as a parent. They saw only the power struggle and not the call to the soul of a parent Luke's gospel (2:41-52) recounts this call.

"His parents used to go every year to Jerusalem for the feast of the Passover. When Jesus was twelve, they went up for the celebration, as was their custom. As they were returning at the end of the feast, Jesus remained behind, unknown to his parents. Thinking he was in the party, they continued their journey for a day, looking for him among their relatives and friends. Not finding him, they returned to Jerusalem in search of him. On the third day, they came upon him in the temple sitting in the midst of the teachers, listening to them and asking them questions. All who heard him were amazed at his intelligence and answers. When his parents saw him, they were astonished, and his mother said to him: "Son, why have you done this to us? You see that your father and I have been searching for you in sorrow." He said to them: "Why did you search for me? Did you not know that I had to be in

my father's house?" But they did not understand what he said to them. He went down with them to Nazareth and was obedient to them. His mother meanwhile kept all these things in her heart. Jesus for his part, progressed steadily in wisdom and age and grace."

It is by no means a coincidence that the only account we have of Jesus as a child is when he was approaching adolescence. If there was ever a time that parents needed divine inspiration and guidance, it is when they are parents of an adolescent child. Even God's son exhibited the stereotypical rebellion, posturing and search for independence so much a part of adolescence. And as for his parents, well, some things never change. Just like us, they worried over the behavior of their adolescent child. Their firm but slightly insecure admonition was so much like ours. We know what is best, but our teenagers seem so sure of themselves and so determined to do things their way, we often find ourselves questioning our own judgment. Like Mary and Joseph, we must be firm in our commitment to continue to be parents to our adolescent child.

The symptoms of this adolescent age are universal. Bubbly conversations are often replaced with monosyllabic grunts and caustic retort to simple parental questions like "How was your day?" Adoring eyes often turn to glaring slits in a pouty face. These budding adults vacillate between the worlds of adulthood and childhood. At such a precarious juncture, what they value most they seem to vigorously reject. Our children have always needed our love, support and guidance. Now, in spite of their words to the contrary, they need it even more than ever. At a time when they may seem most unlovable, they need to experience our love more than ever. Do not, in spite of what they say or do, as they grow older, eliminate established patterns of family behavior from their daily lives. Rituals are very important to the adolescent. They signify acceptance and belonging. Instead, modify their role in family and traditions to fit their present situation. Adolescents should not be allowed to exclude themselves from family rituals. They should instead, be given a more adult, a more responsible and active part in them. We must help them learn how to be an independent person who is still an active member of a family. Don't let them exclude themselves from their greatest support system, their family.

It is never easy being a parent. But, being a parent of an adolescent is particularly trying. It has always been a source of strength for me to recall how Mary and Joseph handled their rebellious teen. They grounded him for eighteen years. They must have. The next time we hear of him he is thirty years old. That might not work well for you. But at least trust your same God-given intuition. Claim for yourself what we behold in Mary and Joseph. Parent your child so that he/she too will continue to grow in wisdom and age and grace.

~

A Family's Response

"How could God let this happen?" I cannot even begin to count the number of times I have heard this heart-wrenching cry from someone desperate to make sense of a painful reality. I cannot even count the number of times I have said it myself. Just this morning I said it when I heard, once again, of the sudden death of a child. I say it to myself every time I think of the holocaust of abortion. I think it every time I read of child abuse or the growth of the sub-culture of violence. I heard it over and over again following the terrorists attacks on September 11th. Does God really let these things happen? No, I think not. But it is God who gives us the strength to respond in faith when they do happen.

God is good. Evil in any form is not of God. God does not test our faith. He knows we have faith. Only the devil tests your faith. What a coup it is for Satin to gather us into his camp by blaming God for the tragedy and sadness in our lives and in the lives of our families.

We hear a great deal about the weakness of the family structure today. But there is an underlying strength in every family that can be brought forth. Strength implies fitness and readiness. How does a family prepare to be strong? How have we become fit enough to be counterculture? When our family experiences loss, separation, divorce, death or children in crisis, how will we, as a family respond? Looking to God for individual and family strength is an empowering way to avoid the pitfalls of material measurements that get us thinking in terms of good families and bad families and judging one family against another. All families have struggles. Public or private, all families have problems and crisis. Support for each other that begins with prayer is a God-centered response that conveys family spiritual fitness.

I read a frightening statistic the other day. When asked in a questionnaire if they prayed together at home as a family, 84% of students in a national survey responded 'no'. And we wonder why there are problems in families. Did God let this happen, or did we? I know that prayer seems like a simplistic answer. I know that prayer takes away our feeling of control. I know that prayer does not always give us the answer we want. But through prayer, God gives us what we need. He gives us the strength and courage we need to discern the truth. He gives us the will to survive. He gives us the vision and hope we need to recognize an even greater good. To begin to understand and to demonstrate through family prayer the strength of your spiritual fitness is to begin to exercise your God-given power and authority to destroy evil and see it gradually disappear from your experiences.

God does not will the evil that attacks us. But God is with us when it does and will protect and strengthen us if we but ask him. Tonight, as family, whatever structure your family takes, say one prayer together. Commit to a program of family spiritual fitness. It is

then that you will experience what it is that God lets happen.

~

A Grandparent's Role

Recently I became a grandparent. It was the fourth time in a little over a year and a half. My role in this most recent proceeding was to do what grandparents do, baby-sit. I was in charge of my grandson, Nicholas, until his parents returned from the hospital with his baby sister. My daughter left pages of instruction but I never had time to read them so I resorted to a grandparent's right to take the path of least resistance. It is a luxury not afforded to parents. By the time the rest of his family returned home, Nicholas was a changed man. He had rediscovered the unrestricted use of a pacifier. He kept one in his mouth and a spare in each pocket. He had a bath in the sink, frozen yogurt and Cheetos for dinner and stayed up until ten while waiting for his favorite blanket to dry. I am sure his parents will straighten him out as their routine returns. As for me, I have learned what a grandparent's role is really about.

It has never been easy being a parent. But, being a grandparent or a great grandparent of a child in today's society is a particular challenge and a particular delight. My grandchildren don't fool me with their charming theatrics, but I find it entertaining that they try. It didn't take long before they learned that I am a "soft touch" and on more than one occasion we have become co-conspirators in getting around their parents' rules, like "Finish your dinner, or no dessert". I am delighted that they are always so eager to see me. Their faces light up when I open my front door and they bound into the house with the expectation of a good time. All that I learned about parenting seems not to apply to grandparents so I leave the hard part to their parents. Going to Mimi and Pop Pop's house is an adventure in freedom. Yet, I know that grandparents are supposed to be noted for the things they teach their grandchildren. What can I teach them that will last longer than a good time? What is my role? What example can I give them that will last a lifetime? I know. I will respect and support the wisdom of their parents.

Parenting has become so complicated in today in a society that often seeks to undermine our core values and negate the role of parents as the first teachers of their children. I don't think parents always get the credit they deserve for the strides they are making in raising parenthood to an art form. I remember when mothers had babies and expectant fathers sat around in smoke-filled waiting rooms with a roll of dimes clutched in one hand and a list of names and phone numbers in the other. They waited for the results of a very mysterious process to be announced so they could make their phone calls, pass out cigars and then go back to the business of running the world. Parents today have dismantled the former social order by declaring that parenthood is a joint project. Both mothers and fathers "deliver" their babies and share in the responsibility of childcare in every area from diaper changing to carpools, from cooking to coaching. In a world that often denies the power of family, parents work together to provide for their children the value system they believe will help their child become a God-centered, successful, happy and productive member of society. And, as if that weren't enough, both mothers and fathers go about the business of running the world. They even replaced the cigars with no-smoking signs.

I admire their involvement and am in awe of the energy level of parents today. I am also puzzled by their inability to appreciate just what an outstanding job of parenting they do. I have spent most of my life with other peoples' children and I have seen the fruits of their labors. If there were only one thing I could say to parents today it would be this, "Never doubt your God-given ability to be a loving, successful, effective parent. You have the ability to be a parent who knows that there are good times and bad, laughter and tears, that an appropriate "no" is more loving than a million "yeses," that right is still right even if nobody else does it, and wrong is still wrong even if everybody else does it, and that God is the source of our strength. When there are times you feel lost, pull over and ask God for directions. He will give you what you need to continue the journey. All of us grandparents and great grandparents, all of us who have been where you are, all of us who have raised you, all of us are here, first to support you, then to play with your children. When you can let go of the fear of failure, the fear of comparison, the fear of inadequacy and the fear of imperfection, then you can love joyfully and freely and truly appreciate the God-given gift of parenthood and the wonderful job you are doing. You will also be able to look forward to that blissful time when the pressure is off and you can let your grandchildren eat frozen yogurt and Cheetos for dinner."

~

A New School Year

Forget the calendar. Forget the thermometer. Summer ends when we are barraged with back to school ads. When I was a child, the few weeks before school started rivaled the Christmas season. It wasn't that I couldn't wait to get back to the classroom. What I was really looking forward to was the newly sharpened pencils, the new school bag, new notebooks and a new beginning. Each new school year brought the excitement and enthusiasm of learning something new. Each new school year was going to be the year I would keep everything in order, read extra library books, do all my homework and really pay attention in class. It was just like a New Year's resolution, and lasted about as long. But, every year, it wasn't long before I lost my pencil somewhere in the bottom of my book bag along with my homework. The library books were overdue before I finished them and the person in the desk next to me was always more interesting than the teacher. Somehow, having all the new things needed to start a new school year leads students to believe that their education isn't about them, its about all the "stuff" they need to take with them. And when the all the new "stuff" gets old, what is it they really need to keep the enthusiasm and excitement for learning alive?

Before you know it, it will be that time of the year when the newness and high expectations of the first day of school have been replaced by the reality of the day to day. The pencils aren't quite as sharp, the book bag is a little less organized, and the shoes are not as shinny. But the enthusiasm should still be there with the excitement of learning something new each day, regardless of report cards or parent teacher conferences. How can parents maintain that level of enthusiasm for children, while at the same time make a realistic evaluation of their progress, and not equate, for better or worse, the child with the grade?

For as long as schools have existed, there have been methods for reporting to parents about the progress their children make in school. All of the methods involve assigning a mark that indicates a level of progress so that parents could understand clearly the progress their children are making in school.

It is unlikely that a grade reporting system will ever be devised that is so precise that there can be universal agreement on just what a grade means. To some parents, a "B" on a report card means that their child is doing very well in school. Other parents may feel that nothing less than an "A" denotes satisfactory progress. The grading system a school uses will be much clearer to you once you understand the elements that usually go into determining the grade a student receives. In deciding upon a grade, a teacher considers many objective factors. These factors include the grading standard the school has established, the ability of all the students in the class, the achievement of a student in relation to his/her identified abilities, the expectation the teacher has for a student, and the progress the student makes in a given reporting period. The report card grade is affected by all these factors and teachers consider them as objectively as possible when assigning a grade. There are also some subjective factors to consider as well. The most important are the student's attitude and behavior while he/she is in school. While attitude and behavior do not unduly influence a grade for achievement, they are important factors to consider. The effect of appropriate behavior and a positive attitude go a long way to help a child achieve. Because grades contain both objective and subjective elements, we should view them as general indicators of progress at a particular time. Report cards are benchmark performance evaluations. If the performance is not up to the ability or expectations of your son/daughter then you and the teacher should discuss the situation together, with the best interest of your child at heart.

When my children were young and learning new skills, I was inundated by the "Mom, watch me!" They were excited about learning and wanted me to appreciate, however unskilled, their attempts. Report cards are another way of saying, "Mom/Dad, watch me!" Watch me grow, watch me learn. Appreciate my progress. Keep me enthusiastic about the excitement of new beginnings, of a new school year, even in the middle of winter.

~

Your Child Is Watching

Your child is watching. What is your child learning from you? What is your child learning about being an adult, a parent, a spouse? What is he/she learning about righteousness and compassion; about courage and faith; about gentleness and strength; about joy and sorrow; about laughter and tears? What is your child learning about stress and enjoyment; about right and wrong, about virtues and values? Parents, work had to give children all the best life has to offer. We want to give them all the right stuff. Regardless how much we give them, we cannot give them the perfect life. We are not perfect. Why, then, do we constantly strive for that perfection for our children? What are they learning from us?

Parents often find themselves keeping a fearful vigil over their children lives. It is as if letting our guard down, even for a moment, will cause everything to crash and we will somehow fall short as a parent. Constant striving for perfection in our parenting, or in our children, only causes rage, exhaustion and guilt. We begin to second-guess our every decision. When we are at work we think about the child, at home we think about our work. At rest we think about the commitments we made, when over-committed, we think about the rest we need. We can never move forward in any area of our lives if we constantly run in a circle. Your child is watching, what is your child learning from you?

Parents have great hopes and wonderful dreams for their children. Can we pay the real price to fulfill the dream of a life well led? Can we endure the labor involved? Will they see in us the example for their happiness? Can we trust that suffering, theirs, and ours have its place and that struggles are woven into the fabric of life? Can we accept our children for who they are? Do we have the courage to accept the incredible magnitude of our significance in their lives? Your children are watching. What are they learning from you?

Parenthood is a journey, not a destination. When too preoccupied with keeping away all that might go wrong with our children, we miss all that is going right with them.

Allow yourself to relax and experience the joy of being a parent. If trials come, you will be able to handle them. The world may give parents a hard time, but God loves them. He is always with parents in their needs. Do not fear your child's next stage. Do not anticipate the possibility of failure. Enjoy and learn from the stage he or she is in now. Recognize the power of your example in the life of your child. What you are, your child will become. Show him/her how to be a strong, a loving, and a wise parent. Our children are watching. What are they learning from us?

~

Strengthen The Human Chain

When I was growing up, my family would spend the summers at the beach. Learning to swim in the Atlantic Ocean also meant learning to respect the unpredictability of the undertow. I learned that respect after I was pulled from its' grasp by the last person on a human chain of rescuers, as I was sucked under the water for what I thought would be the last time. It was an experience I did not want repeated. I had a choice to make. I could stay on the safety of the shore and insure that it would never happen again. Or, I could become a stronger swimmer and prepare for the risk. I chose the latter.

How many times in our parenting have we faced choices that have the same effect on us? How many times as parents have we felt "pulled under" by the pressures from peers or the media or by the arbitrary dictates of a secular society? We fight to keep our head above the "water" of opinions and do what we feel is right for our children. Yet, sometimes, we feel as if we don't have the strength to hold out. It becomes easier and easier to just give up, to go along. It becomes easier to assign blame and offer excuses. It becomes easier to accept what is morally wrong when what is morally wrong becomes the familiar environment and doing what is right becomes the risk. Parents cannot afford to cling to the perceived safety of staying on the shore, when to do so makes us weak.

Parents have a choice to make. We can just sit on the sideline and watch society raise our children or we can become stronger parents and prepare for the risks that we will encounter. Choose the latter. It is not easier. It will require a lot more strength, self-discipline and patience. But to do otherwise is to deny your ability to parent. We need the strength to unleash our potential to parent. We must have the courage of our convictions and a strong moral code. We need a deep faith in God. And, we need to pray. God has given us inexhaustible reserves of strength and courage through prayer.

There is something else we need. We need each other. Too often we are tempted to just give in to the pressures around us and say, "What can I do? I am only one person." I cannot help but think, "Where would I be had each of the twenty-seven persons on the human chain of rescuers who pulled me out of the ocean felt that way?" No one of them was able to save me by himself without getting caught in the undertow, and suffering the same fate. But, by working together, supporting each other, trusting each other and relying on each other, I was pulled to safety. Maybe we should take the same approach with our children. Maybe we should seek out others who will join with us in rescuing the children from all that threatens them from becoming the person God intends them to be. Perhaps, by working together, supporting each other and relying on one another our children will be pulled to safety. They are not yet strong enough to save themselves. Teach them how to be a stronger person by exhibiting that strength yourself. It is a strength grounded in prayer and faith and a willingness to come together with others who will create a human chain of rescuers.

~

It Takes Time

A few years ago a best selling book, The One Minute Manager, was touted as the epitome of timesaving ideas. Everyone's time is so limited. Everyone has too much to do. In this book, effective human interaction was reduced to a "run and gun" style where everything worthwhile saying could be said in one minute. Other one-minute strategies for a myriad of careers soon followed. But the trend for reducing communication to sixty-second maximums hit a new low when the One Minute Parent hit the shelves.

I have only one response to the "one minute" theory. The results of the reality check are in. There are no quick fixes. There are no shortcuts through parenthood. Being a one-minute parent might be a short-term survival strategy, but with enormous long-term costs. We reap what we sow. Time is a seed of love. When you sow time into your family, you'll reap love. Jesus taught that giving was the beginning of blessings, "Give and it shall be given unto you." (Luke 6:36) A one-minute parent will raise a one-minute child. Then, in the context of our hectic, crowded, over-committed culture, the foundations of our interpersonal relationships, the foundation of our family structure, the foundations of our vocation as parents, will be destroyed in our inability to be truly present to another person.

Louis Pasteur, the French scientist, expressed a philosophy relevant even today when he said; "When I approach a child he inspires me in two sentiments.

Tenderness for what he is and respect for what he may become". What he or she may become depends on what parents do now. The first step toward success in encouraging that future greatness of a child is the willingness to listen now.

If you think you're pressed for time, remember, there were not too many people busier than Christ Himself. He had only three short years to bring the message of salvation to an unbelieving world. He traveled on foot from place to place without benefit of television to spread His message. He gave us a sincere example of sincere communication. He made very clear the tenderness and respect He had for children when, in the middle of a very important gathering, He said, "Let the little children come unto me, for such is the kingdom of God." He recognized the greatness that lay beneath the surface of childhood. He knew the importance of leading the children in the right direction, toward Him. I doubt if He read The One Minute Savior. It takes us more than one minute to raise a child into the kind of adult who can raise a child. It takes time. If you have only one minute to give your child, I suggest that you use that minute to reevaluate the priorities in your life. It will be the best minute you ever spent.

~

SECTION TWO:

A LIGHT REFLECTED

IN

A LIFE WELL-LIVED

The Arms Of God

Miracles happen! They are the swaddling clothes of our daily lives. They are God's whispers of faith and hope and love that come to us all if we are listening. In this season of miracles, I share such a whisper with you.

We live in a world of gurus and experts. There is a plethora of books; an abundance of workshops, articles, and television shows all proclaiming parenting strategies that work. Maybe they do. More often than not, all this external knowledge never becomes wisdom and transformation. If the strategy is not easy to fit into our daily lives, we never really internalize someone else's solutions. We continue to cling to the notion, however, that somewhere there is an expert who can save us. We are weary of this culture of violence and death. We long for a transformed kingdom on earth. There are times when those who have made peace with the status quo exhaust our vision of what could be. But our vision is about children. Our vision is about an awakening of our spiritual identity. Our vision is a moral quest to reclaim for our children the values, the virtues and the dreams that are their inheritance as children of God. We cannot accept anything less.

In the past few years, my prayers for the children in our society have taken on an urgent tone as the chaos they experience grows. One morning, as I knelt in a church in Memphis where I live, I felt a certain sadness that tempted me to despair those things would never *change. I looked at Christ on the crucifix, His arms outstretched, and thought, "We need you to wrap your arms around your children and protect them, but sometimes it seems as if You have no arms".*

About a month after that morning I was at a conference in San Diego. The group I was with visited one of the old missions. As I knelt in the dimly lit church, I looked up. There, over the altar, hung a large crucifix. The finely carved figure of Christ that hung on the cross had no arms. I was transfixed. Here, thousands of miles from Memphis hung the armless God of my prayer. What a coincidence. Who would hang a broken cross over the altar and why? I asked the priest at the Mission why the figure had no arms and why a broken cross hung so prominently over the altar. He told me he found the crucifix buried under a tarp in the corner of a small shop in Rome. In spite of the fact the arms were missing, the wooden figure of Christ was so beautiful and the look on His face so moving, he decided to buy the crucifix, have it restored and hang it in the Mission. When Father returned to San Diego and the Religious Sisters at the mission saw the crucifix, they convinced him to hang it just like it is, without arms. They said it would remind us that we are Christ's arms and must do His work in the world. What a very clear answer to my prayer. What a loud whisper of hope.

We cannot clutter our lives with more voices telling us how to raise our children. The only voice we need is the one that whispers to our soul, " They are made in the image and likeness of God, to whom else shall you turn?" We turn to God for our answers. Our prayers are an act of faith in the midst of doubt. He will give us the wisdom to discern the truth. He will give us the courage to transform the world. He will give us the strength to take unprecedented action on behalf of our children. He does have arms. They are ours.

~

Programmed For Endurance

Not long ago, while waiting in line at the grocery store, I overheard a very weary-looking young father with a baby in his arms and a toddler in the shopping cart, say to the clerk, "My wife is sick, the kids are sick, the baby was up all night and work is piling up on my desk. I feel like I'm sixty". I looked at him and thought, "No, you feel like you're your thirty, with a family to raise and a thousand bells to answer. If your were sixty, you would have gotten a good night's sleep, wondered if your grandchild's cold had gotten better and your work would be piling up on someone else's desk." Survival has its rewards. But when you are in the midst of the storm, it is sometimes difficult to even imagine that any calm will follow. It will. Just hold on.

The incident reminded me of a time in my life when I was where that young father is. I had children who were sick and had been up all night. I had work piled up on my desk. I had overextended my obligations to church and civic groups. It was two o'clock in the morning and I was baking cupcakes for what seemed, at the time, like a very important event. I found myself thinking wistfully about the last real rest I had. It was when I was under anesthesia having surgery. As strange as it seems, in my exhaustion, came insight. I thought about the times that Christ went off to a quiet place to rest. He programmed His life for endurance. Maybe I should do the same. Perhaps I should trade the excitement of the sprint for the measured pace of the long distance run. If Jesus prioritized the time to rest, leaving thousands of people to be healed, surly I could cut back on a few of the demands on my time, too. If we are always consumed by the things we are doing, then we will lose sight of the person we are becoming.

It takes the grace of God to recognize and treasure the moment we have, no matter how difficult or tedious the moment is. To remain faithful to the day to day is all we are really called to do. There will be times when that faithfulness is challenged. There will be times when the clamor of the demands on us drowns out the whisper of the soul urging us to things eternal. When we try to please everyone, we please no one, including ourselves. When we try to accomplish everything, we accomplish nothing. When we neglect our own needs, we eventually lack the spiritual and physical stamina we need to become the person God intends us to be. We cannot give what we do not have. What is it we need to do in order to meet our challenge of faithfulness to what we are called? Perhaps we need to do what Christ did, rest and pray. It you find these solutions impossible to do, then you may need them more than you realize. In the meantime, we can ease the overburdened life of our families by being sensitive to each other's weariness and by being wise enough to unburden ourselves of our own weariness, so that when we are sixty, we don't still feel like we did when we were a young parent of thirty.

~

Exercise A Miracle

I saw an interesting commercial on TV the other day for a piece of exercise equipment. I knew it must be a major breakthrough by the effortless way in which the announcer could work every muscle without sounding the least bit out of breath, as he raved about the miraculous results that anyone purchasing this equipment would experience. How effortless it all seemed. That was certainly the equipment for me. I was tempted until reality crept in. That equipment would only serve to keep my treadmill, residing upstairs, from dying of loneliness. I have learned that to receive any benefit at all, I would actually have to get on the equipment and do something. The benefits he claimed sounded more like work to me than a miracle. I wanted it a little easier than that. After all, we live in a world that tells us the solutions to our problems are found outside ourselves. If we have difficulties at all it is because we haven't found the right program or product yet. We are not responsible for anything more than patience as we wait for miraculous results.

Oh, have no doubt, miracles do happen. I've seen more than a few. God does provide us with spontaneous enclaves of goodness in the midst of chaos. They occur most frequently as God's response to someone's actions of self-discipline, generosity, courage and prayer. There is a story I heard that speaks to miraculous results.

There once was a King who agonized over the tragedy, the poverty, and the violence in his kingdom. He prayed to God, "Lord, my subjects and I want to transform the kingdom. Is there anyway you could assist us? " God replied, "Yes, would you like me to do it the miraculous way or the ordinary way?' Not wanting to appear greedy the King replied, "The ordinary way". At that very second, God sent legions of angels across the land in response to the King's request. Wars ceased, crops grew and there was so much abundance that everyone worked and prospered. There was peace throughout the land. The king was astonished and said, "Lord, if that was the ordinary way, what is the miraculous way?" "If you would do it yourself," God answered.

God wants us to participate in the miracles of transformation. His miracles came with a call to action first; "fill the jugs with water", "collect the loaves and fish", "Take up your bed and walk". He still calls those in need of a miracle to action.
There are times when a parent feels like that King. There are times when we think there is nothing we can do. The problems seem overwhelming and without solution. There are times when confronting the chaos and complexity will take nothing short of a miracle. How will you maintain your internal resolve and resiliency? The search for insight and transformation is a heroic journey, but the treasure at the end is worth the quest.

For what miracle are you waiting? What is it you are willing to do to ensure the fundamentally good behavior, practices and priorities of yourself and your children? It is never too late for the improvement you want. If it took awhile for circumstances in your life or the life of your family to take a downward spiral, then it will take some time to change it. That kind of transformation of our parenting begins in prayer in patience, and in action. As Mark Twain said, "You can't break a bad habit by throwing it out the window. You have to walk it slowly down the stairs." You have to take action first, and be patient with your progress. Within the vision that drives our action lie the seeds of a miracle.

As for my interest in that latest physical fitness equipment, if I'm still looking for a miracle, perhaps the miracle will be that I actually go upstairs and give the treadmill a workout. Miracles do happen.

~

The Silent Treatment

I heard a story recently about a woman whose husband was dead for three days before she called for help. When the paramedics arrived they asked her why she waited so long to call them. "I didn't realize he was dead", she said. "I thought he was just giving me the silent treatment".

I'm not sure if this is a true story or not but the sad thing is, it could be. Anger isolates. No matter what spin we put on the inability to recognize, communicate and deal with our emotions; it is fool hearty to ignore the evidence of what is really happening. I don't know what that woman did to incur her husband's anger. What I do know is that anger holds us hostage if we stay focused on the behavior of another rather than focus on our own feelings and how to deal with them. What a feat for that man to be so good at not communicating, at not reconciling, at not letting go of anger, that he could slip, unnoticed, into eternity. It's the kind of isolation experienced when we make external things central to the meaning of our lives.

There is a time for anger, a time for calling us, and others, to accountability. But habitual anger is an enslaving traveling companion that seeks to destroy. The only difference between a rut and a grave is the depth. When you focus only on things outside your control, you lose control. Unless we learn to let go of a need to control the behavior of others we will never be free of the anger that controls us. In some relationships, there is a need on the part of one person to blame the other for the anger felt, and an equal need by the other to accept that blame and to try to change to conform to the expectation of the other person. When we become comfortable in an environment of emotional dishonesty in order to survive in a relationship we give up who we are. We give up the person God intends us to be. Our life is about more than just surviving a relationship with another person. Our life is about the inner conversion that transforms us by our relationship with God. If the admission price to a relationship with another person is to deny who we are and give up who God intends us to be, then the price is too high.

Faith is grounded, not in laws, but in a God who loves us, unconditionally. This unconditional acceptance of who I am does not imply approval of all I do. It is a promise of love and the encouragement to grow. When we have the courage to begin the process of letting go of anger we find we become less judgmental of the behavior of others. We also become more forgiving of our own behavior and our self. We let go of the need to be perfect or to expect perfection in others. We come to the realization that it is only with God, through God, and in God, that we are perfected.

I cannot make another person like me. I can only let go of my need to be liked by another person. Handing myself over to the control of another does not guarantee happiness. It only guarantees control. All spirits are entitled to be free. The only approval, acceptance or appreciation we need is found in a view from the cross.

It is a transforming relationship with God that frees us of our anger toward others and our condemnation of their behavior. The ultimate freedom is realized only when we place our life in God's hands and give anger the silent treatment.

~

Thanksgiving For Lessons Learned

Thanksgiving, like truth, is not something finished, but something unfolding as life goes on. I am often reminded of this while saying the Grace Before Meals. I'm saying, "Bless us O Lord, and these Thy gifts, which we are about to receive", and I'm thinking, "What is this that I am about to receive?" So often we don't recognize the blessings we receive because they come hidden only in what we see, or disguised in the lessons we learn. For me, Thanksgiving has always been about thanking God for the lessons I've learned and for those He has sent to teach me. One of those lessons actually happened on Thanksgiving thirty years ago.

My husband, Joe, and I and our two children moved from our hometown to a distant city. We lived in the cove of a street with four other young families, like ourselves, who had been transferred to the area by the companies for whom they worked. All of us were away from our hometowns. Since none of us were able to get back home for Thanksgiving, we decided that it would be a good idea to spend the holiday together. I volunteered our house, for no other reason than that I saw it as leverage needed to get the new den furniture that I had been wanting for some time. It was not as if we needed new furniture, I just thought that what we had wasn't good enough. With all this company coming, what better time to display a new look. Joe had other thoughts on the subject. He decided that this was not a good time at all to invest in furniture. He told me that what we had was indeed good enough, and nobody really cared what they sat on anyway. I thought I needed another strategy. What I actually needed was another lesson.

Two weeks before Thanksgiving, my new friends and I decided to have a Garage Sale. As I was complaining to them about not getting new furniture, I had an idea. I decided to sell the old furniture so that Joe would have no other choice but to replace it. And, with all the company coming, it would have to be purchased before Thanksgiving. The furniture sold. When Joe got home that evening, needless to say, he was surprised to have no place to sit. I told him about my great idea and suggested that we go out shopping for furniture. He didn't say anything, just looked around the empty room. He went to the attic and returned a few minutes later carrying our lawn chairs and placed them around the room. After two more trips to the attic, our den was decorated in an eclectic array of folding chairs and tray tables. I stood there and watched. When he was finished, he looked at me and said, "See, I told you we don't need new furniture. These are good enough, and there are plenty of seats for everyone. At first I thought he was joking. But, as he settled in on the folding lounge chair and read the paper, I could tell he was already comfortable with the new look. His mind was made up, for now anyway.

We didn't talk much about the furniture for a couple days. By the end of the week, our children were heroes. Their friends thought that they had the "coolest" house in the cove. Some even suggested we put the sandbox inside to complete the look. My new friends suggested all kind of decorating tips for when the time came to get new furniture. Joe's friends came just to look, and to ask for his advice. Actually, our den became the place to be that Thanksgiving. Five families, from five different places, with different cultures and histories, came together that day and bonded for life, not by what we had, but by what we had to offer each other, friendship. We ate, we laughed, we told our own "Lawn Chair" stories, the children played without once being told to get their feet off anything, and we thanked God for bringing us all together to be "family" for each other when we were all so far from our homes.

By Christmas we had new Den furniture. As much as I liked it, I sort of missed the lawn chairs. What I kept, however, was the lesson I learned. People are always more important than things, and our most cherished possessions are our relationships.

If we spend as much time nurturing our relationships with people as we do dusting our collections of things, we would become the persons we were meant to be. It is in our relationships with others that we learn who we are and what it is God intends for us to be. It is through others that God sends the lessons we are to learn. If I decorate, not my house, but my life, with my relationships with others, then wherever I am will be home. Every day will be Thanksgiving and I will be thankful for the gifts I am about to receive, however disguised, for I will not receive them alone.

~

A Snake's Tale

If you hear of a contest in the "Well, what did you expect?" category, let me know, I have the winner. I read an article in the newspaper about a man who was almost squeezed to death by his pet snake. Somehow, the boa constrictor worked its way out of its cage in the man's bedroom and wrapped itself around its sleeping owner. The startled man was awakened by the intense pressure as the snake continued to squeeze. His screams alerted his wife who managed to save her husband by killing the snake. The man expressed his sadness and disbelief at the snake's behavior. He was quoted as saying, "He was my friend. What did he do that for?" Friend or not, it was a snake. What did the guy expect?

The article reminded me of a tale I heard years ago, a tale that has, on more than one occasion, allowed me to recognize the contradictions that surround us everyday.
A young girl was walking through the woods on a cold winter day when she heard a voice call out, "Girl, help me! She looked down and saw a snake at her feet. The snake cried out, "Please help me. The ground is frozen and I am cold. If I stay down here I will freeze to death. Please pick me up and put me under your coat. It is warm there." The girl looked at him and said, "No, I cannot pick you up, you are a snake. If I put you under my coat you will bite me and I will surely die." "No", said the snake, "I will not bite you, I promise. I just want to stay warm, and travel through the woods

with you. I am so cold". The girl looked with pity at the snake. He seemed so harmless as he shivered on the cold ground. Although she knew better, she felt sorry for the snake. In the emotion of the moment, she gave in to his pleas. "Alright", she said, " I'll take you with me and keep you warm. But remember your promise." So the girl picked up the snake and drew him to her to keep him warm. As she wrapped her coat around him, the snake bit her. She fell to the ground. As her life slipped away, she cried to the snake, " Why did you bite me? You promised you would not hurt me. You lied to me." "What did you expect?" the snake hissed as he slithered away. "You knew I was a snake when you picked me up."

It happens. Everything we know, all that we believe, is often tested in the only way and in the only time and place available to us. Our test is not in what we believe, but in our response to the contradiction in the present moment, to the temptation before us. What is it that we pick up? What do we draw to us that could corrupt us spiritually, morally, physically or psychologically? Who do we trust not to harm us? What situations do we put ourselves in that will only serve to destroy us? What do we do that makes us less than who we are? How do we rationalize that our destructive associations really won't hurt us or that bad habits are easy to break? Even the perceived comfort of the status quo can fool us into believing that we are in control. Even our best intentions can deceive us. What snakes have we picked up that seek only to steal our spirit, to destroy our families, our children, our community, our world? What is in our society that lures us with lies? How do we keep the snakes at bay?

It is difficult to trust in the unseen when we would rather believe what we see and hear in front of us, even if it is a snake. It is our nature to be comfortable in a world we create for ourselves. Yet it is through that transparent humanity that our light shines brightest. Our struggles are most clearly seen in the light of faith. It is that faith that gives us the wisdom to judge what we see and experience in the light of what we believe. It is faith that takes over when our best efforts fail. We cannot eliminate the contradictions in our world. It is faith that allows us to understand that they exist and that we can live among them without letting them destroy us. What seems like a good thing could be evil. What appears to be counter-culture could be right. It is God's hand that steadies us when we are weakened, or made vulnerable, by the contradictions in our world. He breaks through our routine to remind us that we are ultimately dependant only upon Him. No matter how many snakes cross our path, He gives us the wisdom to see them for what they are, the strength and courage not to pick them up and the grace to draw to ourselves only Him.

~

Pictures Of A Marriage

There is an Irish proverb that says; "Procrastination is a heavy load". I guess I didn't realize just how heavy a load it is until I tried to move the carton holding our family's photos that are "in transition". You know the ones. You had them developed, enjoyed them, passed them around and will put them in an album, someday. In the meantime they reside in a carton. I decided that that someday had come. It was time to update the archives. I started to sort the pictures and pick up where I left off a few years and several special occasions ago. The pictures in our album look like most albums, with one exception; most of the pictures we have from the past few years center on weddings.

Although the moment was captured for several different couples, there was a certain similarity about the photos. The pictures all captured the joy, promise and hopefulness of the moment. But these one-dimensional wedding pictures, while reliving the memory of the day, could never begin to tell the story of a marriage or of the Sacrament of Matrimony. Vows are said quickly, but are lived out slowly. The reception of a sacrament and living it out are two different sets of pictures.

Where are the pictures of the commitment of what it takes to transform a promise into a reality? Where are the pictures of the times in a marriage when actions speak louder than words? Where are the pictures when "For better or worse" turns out to be worse, when "In sickness or health" turns out to be sickness, when "For richer or poorer" turns out to be poorer? Where are the pictures when the vows, spoken quickly, were lived out slowly, but they were still lived out? Where are the pictures of the marriage?

Where are the pictures of spouses making time for each other when there was none? Where are the pictures of the daily triumphs of faithfulness and forgiveness, of trust and patience, of sacrifice and love? Where are the pictures of marriage that welcomes the newborn and the elderly, the wayward adolescent and the terminally ill child? Where are the pictures of the marriage that survives the routine and the chaotic, separation and familiarity, the burden of perfection and the frailty of imperfection, the nightmares and the dreams? How do you photograph short tempers and long memories, compassion and tenderness? The photo opportunities are there in every marriage. We just don't always think to capture the moment of a decision lived out, of a promise kept, of a grace realized. It is in those pictures of the struggles of a lived commitment that God gives us glimpses of His unconditional love.

Pictures of a wedding are usually placed in an album to admire and reminisce. Pictures of a marriage are placed in the heart to grieve over or to cherish. A marriage is a story of vows said quickly and lived slowly. The Sacrament of Matrimony is a chronicle of the graces received that provide the strength needed to develop stability, endure the hardships and rejoice in the blessings. The sacrament lasts longer than the ceremony and provides the graces needed to live out a commitment that transforms a promise into a reality. How do you take a picture of a sacramental grace? I guess you don't. You just have to be there to experience it. It is these pictures of a marriage that fill our lives. The pictures of the wedding only fill our albums.

As for my carton filled with pictures, I think I finally found a way not to procrastinate any longer. I'll call it a family tradition to keep our pictures in a "Transitional Carton" and put off filling the album, again. As for the pictures of a marriage, they continue to fill my heart.

~

The Junk Drawer

It's one of those things that just about everyone has, but is not willing to admit. I know. I have one. Try as I might to eliminate it from my life, I have finally decided to make peace with the fact that I am a "junk drawer" person. It started out as a drawer. It was just a place to put some of the really "important stuff" until I could get to it. In it, I could always find pictures of people waiting for identification, important phone numbers without names, directions to an unidentified place and a jar of baby teeth (my children's, I assume). As our family grew, so did the contents of the "junk drawer".

At different times, I cleaned out the drawer. The contents were accorded the status of "Junque" and relocated to a box. The box eventually became boxes. The boxes became the attic. Now, after almost forty years of marriage, the attic has the potential of becoming an addition on the house in which to store all our "really important stuff".

"Junk drawers" are one thing. If need be, they are very disposable. "Junk lives" are another, very different thing. It seems that today, our lives are stretched thin and often torn apart by being pulled in so many different directions. Living in the moment is more complicated when the demand of the next moment is already upon us. We simply have too much to do. We constantly set priorities. We make decisions about what to do now and what to put in our "junk drawer".

Often, what goes in the personal "junk drawer of our lives" is lost or forgotten.

What have you put in your "junk drawer" lately? What are the priorities you have set by what you do now and what you put off doing? Everything in our lives; our faith, our family, our work, our friends, our health, our solitude is clamoring for our attention. How do we "downsize" when nothing seems indispensable? How do we prioritize when everything seems to be a priority? Or is it? There will always be a great deal to do. There will always be hundreds of hours worth of "should". Since there are still only 24 hours in a day, something is definitely being put in our "junk drawer". Chances are it is what you need most that you are hiding away.

If you always cater to the enormous needs of the many others in your life, it may not be possible to have the inner peace and strength you need to fulfill the promise of your own journey. You cannot give what you don't have. Even Jesus needed time alone for the R&R he found in prayer and solitude. Maybe it's time you put the oxygen mask on yourself first, take a deep breath and use your renewed energy to attend to the priority of yourself.

Breathe in the oxygen of prayer, of faith and of a peace that will give you a right-beneath-the-surface tranquility. It will give you a sense of God's presence. There will still be a lot to do but it will be O.K. when you have placed your life in God's hands to be lifted up and not in the junk drawer to be lost in the clutter of a much too busy lifestyle. It is not selfish to recognize the need for personal rejuvenation and the time needed to become a spiritually strong person. Maybe all the "stuff" in our junk drawers really is important. How will we ever know if we never take the time to find out what the "stuff" really is?

~

Change Your Strategy

Every family has sayings that are passed down from one generation to the next. Words of wisdom that sum up the family's way of maintaining its' identity and values. One used in our family when I was growing up is also the one I resorted to most often when raising my children: "Change your strategy, not your standards".

This saying is especially true during times of transition in a child's development from one stage to the next. These stages are most evident as a child progresses from one grade level to the next. With each stage dilemmas created when a child's increasing desire for autonomy conflicts with the bonds of tradition. As painful as this dilemma is for the child, the dilemma faced by the parent is even more painful. Parents often experience feelings of anxiety and helplessness when established patterns of communication with their child are no longer effective. At no time is this more evident than when a child approaches adolescence.

Adolescence is the bridge between the child and the adult. It is a time of contradiction. The adolescent has a fierce desire to be independent and just as strong a desire for love and belonging. We, as parents, must confront the pain of change by a willingness to adjust our parenting to meet our child's needs. We often create an emotional distance when we use old strategies to work out new problems. There is a need, at this time, to redefine our emotional connection by using strategies that allow us to let go of the child and embrace the emerging adult. We constantly fight a battle of emotions between providing our children with new experiences and protecting them from failure, thus negating the opportunities for growth. We must set the boundaries within which our children grow and at the same time, guide the development of their autonomy by allowing them to make their own decisions within those boundaries. We must find strategies that will help them redefine their role in the family and give them a strong sense of belonging. We, as parents, are their leaders, their guides across this bridge.

This time of transition is just as difficult for your child. The strategies they have used to relate to family, friends, teachers and classmates no longer seem to work for them. The expectations of the adults in their lives may, for the first time, differ from the expectations of their peers.

In the adolescent world, every day at school has the potential of holding all the anxiety of the first day. The rules seem to constantly change during times of transition. When you change your strategies, not your standards, in establishing new rules, procedures, and expectations for behavior, you assist your child in developing new strategies of their own in their interaction with others without compromising their value system. You benefit them by making it possible for them to define themselves not by what happens to them, but by how they respond to what happens to them. New strategies assist both of you to broaden problem-solving abilities and develop an attitude of success.

Make no mistake, it is not easy but it is love that will carry us through. We will try new ideas and new approaches because of that love. We may make mistakes, but we continue to try. We are the ones who must guide our children rationally and judiciously toward autonomy while maintaining the critical emotional connection and continued grounding in values. What an awesome responsibility. What a faith-filled journey! With prayer and God's ever-present help, we will foster the courage to create a better world by giving to the future the children we raise today.

~

A Miracle In Memphis

High drama makes for great movies and TV Soap Operas but it is not necessarily something I would choose to shape the events of my own life. But, during the first few days of February 1996, the unlikely elements of the chaos theory mixed together with the culture of hope to produce, out of apparent disorder, a miracle that seemed to me to rival that of the marriage feast of Cana.

Our daughter's wedding day was herald by the prediction of six to eight inches of snow with freezing rain and ice to be added to the still frozen accumulation already on the ground. In Memphis, even a hint of a chance of snow is grounds for panic. Guests coming from five countries, sixteen states and right here in Memphis operated with the fuzzy logic that grows out of yet unrealized possibilities. We all proceeded. I knew that the drastic changes in plans that might be called for would in no way diminish the young couple's lifelong commitment to each other. But, of all the possible outcomes to any wedding, I would have gladly traded snow in Memphis for running out of wine in Cana. There was only one thing to do, pray. Pray for that enclave of goodness in the general chaos, a miracle.

It was through prayer that I could let go of possible outcomes and embrace the impossible. If Jesus chose a wedding at which to perform His first miracle, then perhaps He would choose a wedding to perform one now. It was at His mother's suggestion that he changed the water into wine at Cana. I believed that through prayer, Mary would suggest that her son change six to eight inches of snow into a sunny day. So I prayed, "Tell Him they have no sun."

On February 3, 1996, there was a miracle at another wedding feast. In spite of the fact that record-breaking winter storms engulfed the country and snow and ice surrounded the city of, there seemed to be a wall around Memphis and the 100% prediction did not come true. The sun came out. It melted the ice and the hearts of anyone who did not believe in miracles. It was a beautiful day for a wedding. It was a dramatic sign of life and hope in the dead of winter.

God's miracles are not limited to weddings. We limit our chance to experience His miracles when we deny our culture of faith and hope and prayer. This story is not about weddings but about the importance of that faith and hope and prayer in our everyday lives. Now is the time to rekindle their importance and to reclaim our heritage as people of Faith. Make prayer a part of every day. Pray for the strength to honor the absoluteness of the marriage vow. Pray for the fortitude to parent your children grounded in wisdom, truth, and love. Pray for the courage to exemplify for others the constancy of the values of family life and to encourage others by your example of faith and hope. Pray for the acceptance of the possible and the impossible, the likely and the unlikely. Pray for the wisdom to give God the final decision on all our plans. I cannot begin to understand the depth of the mystery of God's ways in our lives. I only know He loves us, delights in doing things for us and ask nothing more than trust from us. We all have stories of God's surprises, His miracles, in our lives. Freely share your miracles. There are plenty more where they came from.

~

The Bully

There is growing concern about overt or covert peer abuse that is bullying. This issue has found its way into mainstream consciences. The light of truth is being shed on behaviors that deny the dignity and seek to destroy the spirit of another. Peer intimidation, whether physical or emotional, is a learned, destructive tactic. It is not surprising that it is becoming more prevalent when current TV shows often glorify negative alliance building and subterfuge. What will one person do to another in order to win? How will one person crush the spirit of another? We easily recognize the stereotypical playground bully who takes particular delight in pushing someone off the swing or knocking another into a locker. Often what we don't recognize as quickly is covert aggression. That's the type of clandestine behavior that turned Palm Sunday into Good Friday. It is the type of behavior that seeks to destroy goodness.

Alternative aggression happens when one person, usually motivated by jealously or a fear of rejection or failure, creates a hostile environment for an unsuspecting victim for nothing more than being a perceived ego threat. The thinking behind this behavior is that by putting someone else down, the emotional bully will raise his or her own status or secure a position in a group. As a teacher, I sometimes saw the way those who practice social cruelty seek to devour their prey. These behaviors, if ignored, continue throughout the bully's life. The only difference is that with age, the bully gets better at the subtleness of relational aggression. An emotional bully's power lies in the ability to maintain a façade of innocence, even persecution or injustice, while manipulating the consensus among a group of often unwitting co-conspirators. This type of bully never operates alone, but hides in a group, seeking the support of those who will often do the "dirty work". Meanness is justified. The alternative aggression that attacks another's self esteem or status, such as negative alliance building, the "silent treatment", isolation, rumors or gossip, persists unquestioned. For the victim who is being shut out by a group, there are feelings of helplessness and doubt. The victim begins to question what he or she could have done to cause this negative behavior in others. If adults have a difficult time dealing with covert aggression in the marketplaces of their lives, how can children be expected to deal with it in the classrooms and playgrounds of their lives? How much longer should this behavior be tolerated, be seen as a right of passage, or accepted as the way things are?

I remember one day after school, a bright, attractive, talented young girl sat in my classroom fighting back tears as she tried to figure out what she had done to cause a team she was on to turn so cruelly against her. She told me about her experiences that fluctuated between isolation by the team, to being invited to a "sleep-over" only to be ridiculed and maligned by the group. My heart ached for her. I asked her, "Why would you want to be on a team that treats people the way you are being treated?" She lowered her eyes and whispered, "What else can I do?" How could I help her? I realized that none of her friends on the team were secure enough to speak out in her defense for fear that if they did, they might be the next victims. A bully understands the power of a conspiracy of silence. What could I say to help her recognize that she did nothing wrong? She was negatively affected by the social problems of another. What could I do to help her become more resilient?

Experience taught me that these behaviors are not confined to any one place or group of people. What could I say to her to help her recognize that what seemed to her to be abandonment by her friends was actually emotional abuse at the hands of a ringleader who was jockeying for a position of control? What did she need to hear from me to be able to speak the truth and discover the exhilarating freedom of honesty? How can a parent or a teacher keep a child from falling into that black hole?

This student took the first step. She sought help. Listen to your children and be aware of their relationships. Give them opportunities to develop many interests and meet other people. Help them express what it is they are feeling. We must name the behaviors that are eating away at the emotional well being of our children, recognize them for what they are and participate in eliminating them. Only God knows the duration and intensity of our trials and only God's grace will give us the courage we need to withstand them. Use His grace to continue to shed the light of truth on all that robs us, or our children, of His peace.

~

What's In A Name?

What's in a name? I know William Shakespeare thought he answered that question when he explained that a rose by any other name would smell as sweet. What he didn't mention, however, was that once that fragrant flower had a name, that name evoked feeling and aroused the senses in anticipation of the scent of the rose. Every name has the same power to create associations and define standards. Advertisers capitalize on that power. There really is a lot in a name. What about your name? What are the feelings, the standards and values associated with your name?

Perhaps I am so keenly aware of the power in a name because it was so much a part of my formative years. From the time I can remember, my parents, in order to set the standards and define the values and expectations of my family, used our last name, Crowley. There were no long explanations or rationales that could compare to the strength of being reminded of what it means to be a member of my family. If ever we dared ask why we should or should not do something, the answer was always the same; "You are a Crowley, that's why". You can't argue with that kind of thinking and you can't buy that kind of pride. Your family name mattered. It was my responsibility to live up to it. It was self-esteem building at its best. It did not mean that the rules were never broken or any easier to follow, but it left little doubt that following them was always in my best interest. To be a member of a family means to be a part of its life, its celebrations and joys, its trials and sorrow, its day-to-day sameness and its unexpected adventures. For children there is a great deal of security in belonging, valuing and being valued.

Family defines who we are and what we value. When a family celebrates together it heightens a sense of pride. A family's celebration highlights the standards, expectations and responsibilities that define what it means to be a member of the family. They all know that they belong and they like it. This internalization of belonging to something of value is a great source of joy and self-esteem for all.

What about your family? What does it mean to be a member of your family? What is the anchor of your family's strength? What standards and values are your hallmarks? Do your children really know what it means to be a (your family name here)? Have you defined your standards so well that just saying your last name evokes an association with your values? What does it mean to be a (your family name here)? Have you stamped your heritage with labels that diminish expectations or define them? If the answer is a little vague, then perhaps it is time to have your own family celebration. Celebrate your history! Celebrate your values and heritage with all the enthusiasm of a pep rally! Let the world know what being a member of your family means! It's the kind of pride you can't buy, but the feeling you instill is powerful. Go ahead. Celebrate. After all, you deserve it, you're a (your family name here)!!!

~

Ask The Question

When Johnny Carson hosted The Tonight Show he sometimes played a character called Carnac the Magnificent in a comedy routine. Carnac would hold a sealed envelope to his head and, after a few seconds of pensiveness, give an answer to a question he had not yet seen. He would then open the envelope and read the question. No mater how bizarre or ridiculous his answer, Carnac always made the answer fit the question; a question he never asked. Laughter was the response from an appreciative audience. That was comedy. The corresponding tragedy is that people give answers all the time to questions they never ask. The results are neither appreciation nor laughter. Having an answer before asking a question makes for a great comedy routine, but not for a great relationship or a better understanding of another person. Our answers, without questions, are not a continual series of interaction with another person but rather extensions of our perceptions and our self. We are people of the "quick fix". We want easy answers to complex problems. We are jaded by the 30-minute solution of a TV show. In reality, the journey of a family, like that of a person, takes a lifetime to travel.

There are times in all families when relationships are strained. There are times when a child or spouse seems to reject the established family values. There are times when a physical, spiritual, emotional or personal crisis of one member tears at the fabric of family life. It is a dangerous practice to assume the answer. It is a dangerous practice to ignore the signs, however subtle or blatant, of changes in behavior or attitude. It is a dangerous practice to pretend all is well and hope for the best. It is not heroic to suffer in silence if the suffering really lies in the soul of another. It is a dangerous practice to have answers when no questions have been asked. As risky as it may be, the courageous will ask the question first. A problem cannot be addressed unless it is identified. Without information we might be tempted to attack the person instead of the problem. We should learn the value of seeking to understand a person first rather than just fixing a problem. Our question is an entry point into the life of another. All too often the breakdown of a family happens when members are operating out of their assumptions rather than seeking the truth.

When I was a teacher, I overheard a student discussion before class. One of the teens bemoaned the fact that her parents were always "bugging" her with their questions. They always wanted to know where she was going and with whom. All the others made a great show of consoling her; all except one. One girl, the epitome of adolescent entitlement, well known for not answering to anyone, said, " Well, at least you know your parents love you". She was right. The other girl's parents loved her enough to question her, to explore the answers with her and to risk her wrath for the presumed invasion of privacy. They loved her enough to notice her and take the time to really know and understand her. They loved her enough not to take the outcome of her life for granted. It takes time to ask the question. It takes time and effort to listen to the answer, especially if in that answer we find we are part of the problem or a cause of the pain. It takes time. But, aren't they worth it? Aren't we?

By asking the question we provide an opportunity for others to reveal themselves to us as we also learn more about ourselves. In asking the question we must be willing to risk owning the answer and giving up our perspective of reality. For in an answer lays the truth about our self as experienced by another person. There are some who would rather cause another person pain then see that truth about themselves, so they never ask the question. When we let go of a need to protect our self or to have a competitive advantage over another or use guilt to make answers fit, we can risk asking the questions first and responding in love to the answers given. The question of the quality of family life cannot be answered until the question of the quality of the life of each member of the family has been asked. Not asking denies us of a dimension of understanding that allows us to bridge the emotional boundaries that create distance between one another. To recognize the pain in another, regardless of how it is manifested, and to be willing to ask the question, is to provide an opportunity for God to work through a person or a situation.

The next time you encounter a person, family member or otherwise, whose change in attitude or behavior seems to cry for attention to a need, be (your name) the Magnificent, open the envelope first. Ask the question.

Wait patiently for the answer. Listen carefully and intently. Respond with love. It might not make the best comedy routine, but it will make a great routine for a life well- lived.

~

Your Field Of Dreams

A few years ago, the movie, Field of Dreams, captured the imagination, and filled us with a wonderment that usually consumes us as children. The story centered on a struggling Iowa farmer who hears a mysterious voice in his cornfield telling him to replace part of his crop with a baseball diamond. Once completed, the field will be the site of a magical meeting of the games heroes from the past. The skeptical farmer was assured that once built, the Legends of the game would come. He built it, and they came. Against all odds, in spite of criticism, ridicule and rejection, he followed the dream whispered to his heart. And when he did, he liberated others to dream, too. If you saw the movie, you no doubt remember that haunting refrain that seems to speak to a need in all of us; "If you build it, they will come".

What is your field of dreams? What is it that you need to build in your lives to have your dream realized? And in realizing your dream, who will come? As, parents, it is our children who will inherit our dreams. What will you build for them? What will they inherit? Do you immediately think of those tangible assets to be amassed before our demise? Perhaps you envision your grateful children when the Will is read and the worldly goods divided. Actually, I don't know how grateful my children will be when they inherit my attic. But our possessions are not the real field of dreams to be harvested. They are not what last.

My dream for our children is a dream I know I share with you. It is not about building things, but about building family. Its value is beyond measure. To build a family is to build a place where dreams are shared. It is a place where each person will learn about himself or herself. It is a place where each person will feel loved and valued and learn that lasting happiness comes from respect for and service to others. Each will grow at their own pace and in their own way, in faith and wisdom and courage. In spite of the family's structure or trials or life circumstances, each will come to realize that family is a place of strength and comfort. It is a place of encouragement and truth, of discipline and patience, of acceptance and challenge. Real family is a safe place in which to grow. It gives us room to experiment with whom we are, to make mistakes and learn from them. It is not a place of being, but of becoming. It is not about what you are but about the limitless possibilities of what you can be. It is an inheritance of faith and values that we build when we build family. It is only with God's help that we can build this field of dreams. It is His voice that whispers to us, "If you build it they will come", not to a place, but to the realization of the importance of family. It is worth more and will last longer that anything else you build. And for generations to come, as your descendents bring the past to life in their families, what they will recall will be the harvest of what you sow in your dreams today. If you build it they will come. Build family.

~

The Perfect Gift

Are you looking for the perfect gift for your child? I have a suggestion for a gift that will be perfect for any child of any age. Give your child hope.

Hope grows out of a sense of security and acceptance. Hope is not a feeling, it is an action. Hope is a gentle persuasion that encourages the heart of another, that pumps oxygen into the soul. Children need a future orientation, an ambition to greatness. Treat your children as if they were already what they could potentially be. If we only recognize the person we see, then we devalue the potential of what that person could become. When you believe in people, they do the impossible. Believe in your children before they succeed, before they even believe in themselves. Your belief gives them hope.

Everyone has seeds of greatness within. When you believe in someone, when you give a person hope in what is yet to be, you water these seeds and give them a chance to grow. They will bloom, in the own time, at their own pace, in their own way.

When your children were learning to walk, your patience, excitement and encouragement made them believe that they would be successful. Even the most tentative attempt was rewarded. You didn't see them toddling. You saw the, in your mind's eye, playing soccer, dancing around the room, walking down the aisle. Look at your children now. What is it they are trying to become? Can you help them keep their dream alive? Can you give them hope?

What do I know about hope?

When I was in the fourth grade, I was painfully shy. I didn't think I was particularly good at anything. Since I was pretty far down on the sibling list, it seemed all the really great things were accomplished by the time I came along. Then, I was assigned to Sister Marie Concilie's class for fourth grade. That made all the difference. Sister seemed to zero in on each student's talent. She made us believe that if she recognized it, then it was really there. She convinced me that I could write interesting stories, that I could speak in public, that I could make people laugh. Every six weeks, when she changed the seat assignments, she put me next to my latest fourth-grade-type heartthrob, whether he liked it or not. She believed in me so I believed in myself.

When I was in fifth grade, Sister was transferred to another school. I never saw her again. I thought of her often over the years. With each accomplishment, I thought of her belief in me. About a year ago, I met a Religious Sister, Sister Deborah, in the same Community as Sister Marie. I inquired about my former teacher of fifty years ago, and learned that she was still alive, although very ill. I got Sister Marie's address and wrote to her that night. I sent her articles about the Catholic schools in Memphis. I told her that due to her influence, I am now the Superintendent of

Catholic Schools and still believing in the gifts she told me that God gave me. I thanked her and told her she was welcome to the credit, or the blame, of what I was doing. One evening, a few weeks later, I got a call from Sister Deborah. She told me that Sister Marie died that morning. She also told me how much happiness she got from my letters and the joy she experienced from hearing from a former student after so many years out of the classroom. It validated her life and her commitment to God to educate. She drove the other Sisters a little crazy those last few weeks of her life, talking about "her" accomplishments in Memphis. Sister left me with one more lesson in hope. I always hoped that I would have the chance to thank her. Once again, Sister believed in me.

Give someone the gift of hope. It's a perfect gift, and lasts a lifetime.

~

SECTION THREE:

A LIGHT REFLECTED

IN

A JOURNEY HOME

Something Is Missing

There is a world beyond our comprehension where reason steps back and the heart takes over. It is a world where wonder and wisdom meet. It is a world of faith. Annie and Jack are twins. They are my grandchildren, born just a few weeks ago, five weeks earlier than expected. Each weighed a little more than four pounds. Annie was fine but Jack had some problems. Jack was taken to the intensive care unit, Annie to her mother's arms. Annie went home. Jack stayed in the hospital. Annie didn't sleep well and Jack didn't eat. He lost weight. When I visited him he seemed restless and I always asked him, "Do you miss Annie?" He would sleep with his arm wrapped around the tiny splint holding his feeding tube.

Several days passed and all Jack's other vital signs were now normal, but he still wasn't eating well or gaining weight. The doctors decided to send him home. They thought that perhaps being reunited with Annie would help. So Jack came home. My son laid him in the infant seat next to Annie. They seemed to sense each other's presence immediately. Annie stopped crying and nestled her head on Jack's shoulder. Jack leaned his head next to her head as if to say, "I missed you". They slept, peacefully. It was as if what they needed most was each other. There had been a piece missing from each of their hearts, shaped in the likeness of the other. Now, they were complete. Jack began eating. They are both thriving.

Jack and Annie's experience is really no different than our own when we sense that something is missing in our lives. There are times when we feel empty or alone and not sure why. Perhaps we feel that something is missing in our family life, in our work, in our relationships or in our marriage. We feel that there is something more that we need, but we don't know what it is. We look for every possibility to fill the void. Often we fill that emptiness with what we think are solutions such as a different job, a vacation, an affair, a bigger house, drugs, more stuff, more money, and on and on. We sometimes even try to fill the void by blaming others for not meeting our need for fulfillment. We are so busy eliminating possibilities we often fail to see the simplicity of the truth. Our adult posturing prevents us from assuming a child-like faith. It is a faith that helps us recognize that there is indeed something more, and that "more" is God. What may be missing in the life we lead is really what is missing in us.

What ultimately completes us, makes us whole, is God. There is a place in our hearts that only His presence can fill. And, when it does, there is no longer room for the restlessness, the need for more, for something else that we sometimes feel. We have all we need to bring our whole self to whomever we are and whatever we do. We can be a complete presence for others. We are content, we thrive, and we are at peace. Like Jack and Annie, we will still have our struggles. But now, we can rest peacefully and assured, knowing that we are

not alone. We are with Him who completes us and we
sense His presence at our side.

~

Raise The Bar On Success

Have you ever noticed how the topic of success has invaded our every waking, and even sleeping, moments? Check out the bookstores, TV Ads, articles in magazines and newspapers. It is easy to find the latest advice or product that helps you be successful at everything from do-it-yourself projects to parenting to saving your soul. Since I have yet to see even one small article or book on how to fail, I assume that we are already well acquainted with that easy task. If I condensed the untold number of strategies for success into one sentence, it would read something like this; "If what you are doing works, keep doing it; if it doesn't work, stop doing it and do something different." As the saying goes, "If you always do what you always did, then you'll always get what you always got." Does this plethora of success oriented self-help material mean that feelings of failure or inadequacy are being promoted to market books and tapes and products of all kinds, or are we just confused as to what success really means.

The truth is, if you are just keeping score, success comes and goes. We win some, we lose some. Maybe it isn't just success we should be seeking, but significance as well. Significance is more than a commitment to success. It is a commitment to the success of others. Success is about who you are. Significance is about whom others are when they are with you. Success is a strategic plan. Significance is a vision.

Whether you are a parent, a teacher or a CEO, your work is not about just being successful or being popular, it is about an obligation to bring out the best in others, to set them up for success. It is not about judging or disciplining others, but about holding them accountable for the decisions they make so that they will grow.

We can be successful and amass great wealth. We become significant by our extraordinary generosity. Success is achievement. Significance is the realization and sharing of God's superabundant graces in our lives. Success could be seen as parenting a child who makes money. Significance is parenting a child who makes a difference. Mother Teresa was not successful in eliminating poverty or disease, yet she was significant in the lives of the poor and dying by giving them aid and comfort. Her significance lives on in the lives of those who continue to carry out her mission of service and her vision of hope.

Success is overcoming your own risks and hardships. Significance is sharing the risks and hardships faced by others. While the fifth consecutive win in the Tour De France by Lance Armstrong, a cancer survivor, is truly astounding, his significance is found in the inspirational courage and determination he models for others who face adversity and challenges in their own lives.

Perhaps, in our own lives, we should not settle for just success. Maybe we should raise the bar and reach for significance, too.

~

Teaching Pigs To Sing

My father has an incredible knack for summing up volumes of an entire philosophy in just one sentence. While I was growing up, I did not always appreciate the wisdom hidden in his advice. In fact, I usually found it annoying and would have preferred that he just give me a straight answer, one I didn't have to think about to ferret out a meaning. But I never could change him or his way of responding. Perhaps that is why I have come to understand, and value, his favorite advice to me: "never try to teach a pig to sing, it will only frustrate you and annoy the pig."

There have been more than a few times in my life that I had to relearn that lesson. It is part of the human condition to be tempted to think that if we just try a little harder, we can change another person. It is not good enough that a person is made in the image and likeness of God, so we set about making someone over in the image and likeness of someone more easily understood, more easily controlled, more like us.

In our relationships, we sometimes find ourselves trying to change someone else to have them behave like us or conform to our expectations. We find ourselves wanting to "fix" another person in order to change a situation. If a relationship with a spouse, a child, a friend, or a coworker, is not working, or is causing conflict, we go to great lengths to find ways to erase the conflict without even identifying its source. We avoid the issue or person, or deny the conflict really exists. Often, we blame other influences for causing the conflict. More often than not, we convince ourselves that if we could just "fix" the other person, the conflict would be resolved. In our quick fix of another, we set about making elaborate rules, structures, and reward systems. We reason, we imply, we command, we exemplify, we preach, we trick, we whine. We do everything but recognize the truth. The truth is that no matter what you do you cannot "fix" another person. If they don't want to change, you can't change them. If they don't want a relationship, you can't make it happen. If they insist on being hostile, you can't make them forgiving. No matter how hard you try, you can't make a pig sing, nor can you make your own song pleasurable to a pig.

Sometimes we know that what another person is doing could be harmful physically, morally, spiritually or professionally to himself/herself or to others. At these times, it is a spiritual work of mercy to admonish, council, or suggest. But none of that guarantees a change in another person. We need to realize that we are not responsible for another's behavior. We are responsible only for how we respond to it. And, in our response, we have a great opportunity to demonstrate true Christian behavior. The heart of our response should be recognizing God's perspective on our relationships or situations in which there is conflict and asking, "What can I learn about myself in this?" Instead of focusing on another person, if we focus on ourselves and our response and look beyond the present situation, we will be able to establish a meaningful connection to another that will heal instead of wound. If there is to be a change, the only one we should be concerned about changing is our self. And that change should liberate the spirit of another.

Often, our only response is prayer. Pray for a change of heart or perspective. Pray for the wisdom to step back and allow another to grow by using his/her own resourcefulness and purpose. When we allow God to work all things together for good we begin to understand that the squeals of a pig may not sound like singing to us, but it does to the pig, and to God.

My father is right. Maybe what will remove frustration from our relationships, what we need to fix most, is our appreciation of the song of another and the way it is sung.

~

The Elevator

It's one of those questions that occasionally crosses my mind when I ride an elevator, or during that two-second delay before the doors open, "What would I do if this thing breaks down and I'm trapped in here?" Last week I got my answer. As I rode alone on an elevator from the top floor of a high-rise office building, I felt an unexpected jolt as the elevator stopped and the doors remained closed. I waited. Nothing happened. The panel light went out so I could not tell where I was on the trip down to the lobby. I pressed the emergency button and every other button I found. I waited. Nothing happened. I used my cell phone to call the office where the meeting I had just attended was held. They assured me that they would contact the management of the building and inform them of my plight. They very kindly offered to stay on the phone until help arrived. I looked at the battery indicator light on my phone and regretfully declined their offer. I called my office to let them know I might be a few minutes late for my next meeting. Time passed with no sign of help. After another call to the office of my prior meeting, I was informed that it would probably take a lot longer than a few minutes to determine exactly where my elevator was, what was wrong and how it would be fixed. I had done everything I could do to help myself. There was nothing I could do to change my situation. I had come to a point where the only thing left to do was respond as a person of hope, that is, to pray and wait. As I waited, I began to think about three persons in my life whose waiting in faith is still an inspiration to me.

I was living in Virginia Beach, Virginia when the American prisoners of war were released from captivity in Viet Nam. Navy Captain Jeremiah Denton was a POW for seven years. I remember talking to him after Mass the Sunday following his return home to Virginia Beach. Our parish had prayed for a miracle, and, here he was, home safely. I looked into his eyes and saw the reflection of God's grace. "How did you get through it", I asked, looking for an insight into his courage. "I prayed and waited for God's time. I never gave up hope", he responded. He placed a horrific situation in God's hands, and waited. Captain Denton was home. He went on to become an Admiral and then a United States Senator from Alabama, all in God's time.

When I was teaching, one of the students in my class mysteriously vanished from her home. An intruder had kidnapped her from her bedroom during the night. For four months her whereabouts, and the circumstances of her disappearance, were unknown to everyone but her and her captor. For all the rest, there were only rumors, false leads, searches, prayer vigils, police interviews, an empty bedroom, an empty desk, bouts of despair and flashes of hope. For four months, fifteen-year-old Leslie Gattas was held captive in the attic of a church just a few miles from her home and a few blocks from her school. Then, as unexpectedly as she had disappeared, she was found. Leslie returned home to a family who never lost hope. I remember the day she returned to school, determined to resume her life where it was so cruelly interrupted. I looked into her eyes and saw the reflection of God's grace. "Where did you find the strength?" I asked, looking for an insight into her perseverance. "I prayed and waited for God's time", she responded. "I never gave up hope". She placed an incomprehensible situation in God's hands and waited. Leslie has gone on to become a successful attorney, a joyful wife and mother, all in God's time.

A few years ago, my dear friends' son, John Rose, was diagnosed with Leukemia. During the months following the diagnosis, John was a patient at St. Jude's Hospital. His treatments left the adolescent athlete weakened and virtually helpless to do anything but wait; wait for the latest medical update, wait for the new protocol to take effect, wait for his life to resume, wait to feel even a little bit better. I sat with John on one of the rare occasions his parents left his side. I remember our conversation. I looked into his eyes and saw God's grace reflected there. "How are you handling this?" I asked, looking for an insight into his determination. "I pray and wait for God's time", he responded. It was a response I had heard before. He placed what appeared to be an insurmountable situation in God's hands, and waited. John is in remission now. He has gone on to graduate from college and he now pursues a successful career in Information Technology, all in God's time.

There might come a time for us, in our vocation as parents, when we find ourselves in a situation that seems hopeless. Nothing we do, or could ever do, can change the seemingly insurmountable circumstances we are experiencing. We have a sense of helplessness as we become more and more dependent on the actions and decisions of others. We wonder if anyone even understands our fears as we reach for even the smallest thread of hope. How do we get through it, the hours, days, or even years of uncertainty? There is only one answer. It is so simple, yet often so difficult to do. We place our situation in God's hands. We pray, and we wait for God's time. We never give up hope.

"Are you OK in there?" "We'll have you out shortly." "Shortly" was much longer than expected, but finally the elevator doors opened. My waiting was over. But the waiting turned out not to be the crisis I envisioned. The waiting was a gift. It was a valuable experience of the wisdom of doing nothing more than praying and waiting for God's time.

~

An Uncertain Journey

It often seems that we spend the first half of our life's journey rebelling against our parents and the second half rebelling against our children. There are times, however, along the road, when all the travelers, weary though they may be, are in agreement as to the route and the destination. For me, Thanksgiving is a celebration of those times and we, the families of today, are the new pilgrims. We attempt to chart a safe passage through a new world that we cannot even imagine. Our feelings mirror the feelings of commitment and uncertainty of those first pilgrims.

The struggles of those first pilgrim families, harsh as they were, do not differ greatly from the struggles experienced by families today. We, like they, know that survival is contingent upon learning to blend the knowledge of our new experiences with the wisdom learned from the past. Our survival includes the survival of our values and family root systems. Each family, regardless of its configuration, has its own unique story and is a unique piece in the mosaic of society. The future of humanity passes by way of a family. Each family's journey is a series of bridges linking generations through the endless evolution of time. The story of family life is the story of love shared, nurtured, rejected or lost as each new generation struggles for its own identity. Yet, in spite of transitions or hardships, people continue to choose to be family. In the haven of that choice, families share the profound and ordinary moments of daily life.

It is difficult for us to imagine how the pilgrim families felt as they confronted their awesome challenges with inadequate reservoirs of experience or resources. They had no books, articles, talk shows, consultants or workshops from which to find solutions to parenting concerns. They recognized their need and turned to the only two sources they knew, God and neighbor. In that insight is the real gift of Thanksgiving. In God they found strength. In their neighbor they found support. Their meal that first Thanksgiving was not so much remembered for the food they shared as for the faith they demonstrated. It was their faith that elevated their souls, enlivened their spirit and gave them the courage to proceed as if limits to their abilities did not exist. They were remembered for their passion for the journey and their trust in God to provide. They were remembered for the gifts they shared and their willingness to reach out to support others on the same journey, regardless of who they were.

Reaffirm the message found in every tradition. It is a message of love that celebrates, in faith, the wisdom of the past and the hope for the future. Celebrate the times your family walks together along the road. Thank God for those who are neighbor to you on your journey. The strength of family values lies in the value placed on family. Take pride in being a strong link in the generation chain of family life.

~

The Original Excuse

I know when it all started. It was in the Garden of Eden. It has come to my attention, however, that it was much more than just the effects of the Original Sin that we inherited from Adam and Eve. We also inherited the effects of the Original Excuse; "It's not my fault". The Original Sin got us into this human condition, but it is the Original Excuse that keeps us there.

God very clearly pointed out a specific tree and instructed Adam and Eve not to eat the fruit from that tree. There was no mistaking this tree for another. God probably posted no trespassing signs all over the place just as a reminder. Unfortunately for us, God finds Adam eating the forbidden fruit. He caught him right in the act, no way out. It was at that moment that Adam initiated our innate desire to cling to the illusion of control over the situations in which we sometimes find ourselves by assigning responsibility for our wrong actions to someone else. First, Adam blamed God, "The woman YOU put here with me, (in other words, if God had not created this other being none of this would have happened). Then he blamed Eve, "... she gave me some fruit from the tree (In other words, if she had not given it to Adam it would have never even crossed his mind to look at that tree). Eve, sensing this new art of ego-preservation, pointed her finger to the next scapegoat, "The serpent deceived me, and I ate, (in other words, the Devil made me do it). (Gen3: 12-13)

It must have been that Original Excuse that incurred God's wrath. It did not come from their offense towards God, but rather the self-destruction that resulted from their disobedience. He already knew they had disobeyed Him before He asked. Parents are like that. They really don't want answers to those "Now what have you done?" questions as much as they want to hear their children accept responsibility for their actions, and perhaps, even apologize. So God did what a parent who keeps His promises does, He followed through with the consequences of their choice, gave them the time and space they needed to learn to accept responsibility for their actions and then, left the light on for their return home; all for the good of His children.

Now, here we are, eons later, still coming up with our own excuses, some quite clever, for not accepting responsibility for our actions. What we need to teach our children, and even learn ourselves, is that we will never be free to try again, to start over, to forgive or be forgiven until we can let go of the Original Excuse, "It's not my fault". The reality is that our society has only succeeded in getting better at pointing fingers. We have raised this culture of blame to an art form. What a list! We blame everything from what side of the bed we got out on, to what kind of day our hair is having. It's not our fault, it's the fault of our peers, our parents, our job, our spouse, the weather, the way we were raised, the person who cut in front of us. It's not our fault; he started it, it's a habit, they lied to me, and, of course, the devil made me do it. Excuses, however comfortable, justified or vindicated they make us feel, don't change anything. They only keep us from starting over, from becoming the person we were meant to be.

So God sent Adam and Eve from the garden, but he sent them off with a memory of peace, a chance to begin again, a reason to change and a new plan for their lives. He knew that in order to start over they needed to be free from the past and live intensely in the present so that they could move beyond their consequences and shame into the freeing power of reconciliation and forgiveness that comes when we accept the responsibility for our actions. It is the same opportunity He gives us. It is a chance to know ourselves better and be better for knowing. I still wonder, though, what would have happened if, when discovered by God eating the forbidden fruit, Adam simply said, "I was wrong, I am sorry. Can we begin again?" I wonder what would happen if we simply said that same thing to someone we have offended, without any excuses.

~

The Conversation Piece

One evening, while visiting with my daughter, she told me that she had been looking for a "conversation piece" for her home for over a year, but still has not found just the right thing. She asked if I had any ideas. Without hesitation, I asked, "What do you want to talk about?" It was obviously the wrong answer. That familiar roll of her eyes indicated that I was clueless when it came to interior decorating. I think she was beginning to be concerned that she might be, too. But then, how could she have hoped to inherit the "Martha Stewart Gene" from a mother whose attempts at gardening are limited to occasionally rearranging the fake flowers in the front yard? As she went on to show me pictures of various "conversation pieces", my mind wandered to the things that started some of the most meaningful conversations in our home when she and her brother were growing up.

The crib was certainly a conversation piece. No sooner did my husband and I place our first child in it when the conversations began. They usually centered on our uncertainty as we ventured into parenthood. "He's been crying for hours, what do you think is wrong?" "I don't hear him, check and see if he is breathing". We would lean on the rails of the crib. Sometimes we would just stare at our son, but mostly we would have conversations about what we wanted his life to be like and what we needed to do to give him that life. However grand our dreams for him, we knew that what he needed most was both of us.

There were lots of things that started conversations when the children were young. Like the things on the floor that weren't supposed to be there; food crumbs, a thousand puzzle pieces, spilled milk, wet towels and too many toys. Those things could always start a conversation. Somehow, those conversations don't seem as significant now as they were then. Clean floors aren't as much fun as the ones strewn with toys. There was, of course, the conversation piece that begged the question, "Whose turn was it to walk the dog?" That piece always started the conversation about responsibility.

As our children entered adolescence, the car keys were always a conversation piece. They were a symbol of freedom for them and a source of concern for us. Their conversations always started with, "Don't you trust me?" And mine ended with, "Love is unconditional; trust, you'll have to earn". It's a difficult lesson to teach and to learn. But children need to learn that trust is a virtue acquired by practicing to be trustworthy. And, while learning, even if they violate the trust now and then, the love is still there. Car keys started many conversations.

The crucifixes over the beds were always conversation pieces. They still are. The conversations are with God. They are conversations that start the day and end it. They are the conversations of parents and children. They are about concerns and gratitude, new jobs and new places to live. They are about death and new life, about changes and stages, about hopes and fears. They are conversation pieces that chronicle the life of a family. Now that I think about it, the most important conversation piece in a home is really the family who lives there.

My daughter pointed to a picture in the magazine and asked, "What about this?' "I don't know", I said, "I kind of like the train set you have on the coffee table. It looks like a family lives here". She just rolled her eyes. I guess I'll never be a decorator.

~

The Anniversary

Not long ago my parents celebrated their 60th Wedding Anniversary. My four brothers and I planned a weekend of surprises and celebrations for them. As I look back on it now, the most memorable times during the weekend, for all of us, were the times we sat around telling "war stories"; who never got caught, who always got caught, who always got blamed, all time greats in the 'Now you've done it' department, and who really threw the football through the picture window-twice. What seemed like disasters when they happened, have now become a source of humorous recollections at family gatherings. And my parents laughed loudest. The experience reminded me of a Mark Twain saying: "My mother had a great deal of trouble with me, but I think she enjoyed it." I would like to think that from my children's perspective, I too, enjoyed parenthood.

Being a parent is never easy, but it is always an adventure. Just when my husband and I mastered one phase of our children's development, they moved into another phase. And, with each child, all the rules were rewritten. I never had the opportunity, or time, to develop a "been there, done that" attitude (except, perhaps, for changing diapers or hearing spelling words). And the adventures kept coming faster than we could keep up with the latest advice on parenting.

The only thing I can assure you, now that my children are adults, is that you are always a parent. Somewhere along the way it dawn on you that you have a lifetime job; that there is no "bringing closure" to this assignment. And when you do realize this, you will be free to relax and enjoy the process. You will learn to make peace with the reality of "in progress" as a permanent state. When you learn that the bottom line is that there is no bottom line, then you will be able to find joy in a job that is not always enjoyable. No one ever said it would be easy, but no one ever said it couldn't be fun either. In spite of crises, illness, trials and tribulations, in a family, regardless of structure, is still the best place to be.

In his gospel St. John says, "There is no fear in love." We should have no fear in parenting because parenting is love in action. Our fears come from our apprehensions, worries and anxieties about the job we are doing. Fears come from our illusions that everything must be perfect or we have failed. They come from a society looking for scapegoats. If we wait for perfection, then we will never be free to love and enjoy doing what we do now. The active love of parenting helps us to move beyond ourselves to meet someone else's needs and follow the greatest command Jesus gave us: to love.

Families aren't perfect, but in the "are we having fun yet?" test, it is more often than not, "yes". One of the greatest strengths a family has is to be able, when in the midst of sorrow, crisis or bad times, to dwell on the good times. Families instinctively dig deep into their reserves of hope, trust, faith, patience and love. I know, for me, dwelling on the good times with my family has renewed my belief that the journey of parenthood has many rewarding and joyful stops. Of course, my parents would still like to know who put the pinholes in the shape of the Big Dipper in their living room lampshades---but we're not talking.

~

A New Year's Resolution

New Year's resolutions are tempting to make, and even more tempting to forget. In spite of the insatiable appetite our society has for self-improvement and excellence, good habits just seem hard to acquire. With the beginning of each New Year, we seem compelled to conquer the past by focusing on the future in at least one resolution. There really is only one. All others pale by comparison. It is to be a person of faith.

Your faith is a gift from God, but others, who are people of faith, nourish it. Seek people of faith. Faith grows out of a lived relationship with a living God. Faith is not an opinion, but an attitude. Faith is not a feeling. Faith is an action. It is a path to be followed. It is a commitment to trust; trust God and the abilities He gave us. Our children learn faith by seeing it lived out in us. They see it when we pray, when we accept God's will for us, when we acknowledge His place in our lives and in the lives of our families. Faith does not answer all our prayers. Faith is our prayers in action. Faith is allowing God to provide the answers to our prayers, in His time and in His way. As others see the fruits of our faith and see the sign of God in our lives, they will understand what faith is. It is more that just a faith expressed. It is the depth of that faith and the joy expressed in living it that makes the difference in our lives. If you want a resolution that really lasts, resolve to deepen the spirit of another by your faith.

What do I know of faith? I have not seen it move mountains. But, I have seen it move people. I have seen it change hearts and lives. I have seen it breath survival into a prisoner of war, and give freedom to a kidnapped child. I have seen it overcome the pain of loss, the agony of a death and the shackles of a life in darkness and despair. I have seen it turn a 100% chance of snow into a warm, sunny day. I have seen it rejoice in the truth, the assurance of God's presence and the knowledge of His providence. I have seen it give rise to the heroes and heroines of character and strength who are unafraid to find joy in praising God and unembarrassed to give witness to His sign in their lives.

With every New Year, every new start, every new idea, the world is waiting, hopefully, for people of faith to lead it. Resolve to be such a person.

~

A Valentine

It is no wonder that time seems to pass so quickly. We live in a society that marks time by card-sending occasions heralded weeks before they arrive. No sooner is the last Christmas decoration put away then the first barrage of red hearts appears. Once again the giving frenzy begins. Although Valentines' Day has become the Super Bowl of the outward display of affection, it pales in comparison to the inner force of love that is quietly lived out day by day, noticed only by those whose lives it affects.

"God so loved the world He sent His only Son." "Greater love than this has no man that he lay down his life". "Love is patient, love is kind". Love is not just a feeling. Love is an action throughout the Bible. God speaks to us of the incredible power of love. Love is God's life in us lived out through our service to Him and others. Love is a power that overcomes hate and causes us to lift up one another. It helps us to continually reach a higher level. Love is faith and hope in action. Love is risking the difficult now for the good of the long haul. Love is doing the right thing, not just saying the right thing. Love is modeling the integrity, honesty and character in ourselves that we want to develop in our children. Love is bringing out the best, even when we only see the worst. It is not easy. Patience is the fatigue on the shoulders of a parent from living that kind of love day after day.

What do I know of love?

I know that it is love that directs the character and shapes the lives of your children. I know that it is love that rocks crying babies and answers a thousand questions from an inquisitive child. I know that it is love that hears spelling words and appreciates a homemade cake with a crack down the middle. I know that it is love that withstands an adolescent's insatiable need to be daring and different and wraps its arms around a wayward child. I know that it is love that reaches out to the lost and the lonely and the painfully shy. I know that it is love that puts a smile on the face of a dying child. It is love that hung on the cross and love that stood at the foot of it. It is love that makes a parent, not a person to lean on, but a person to make leaning unnecessary. Love is the only childrearing theory that works, especially at those times when you feel your child least deserves to be loved.

Are you looking for that Super Bowl of Valentines' gifts? Look no further than that which is already within you. In the end there are only three gifts that last, faith hope and love. And the greatest of these is love.

~

It's Never Too Late To Graduate

Every May I become acutely more aware that we are a people of ceremony and ritual. May is graduation month. Every occasion of transition is cause for celebration, but graduations are special. A graduation is a significant milestone. It heralds a readiness to take on new responsibility with a greater depth of insight of who we are. It is not about being, but becoming. It is about potential that is ready to be tapped, about hope and expectation. All the graduates, no matter their rank in class, in spite of the difficulties they experienced along the way, are celebrated and recognized for their readiness to fulfill their purpose in life. Each is a source of pride to friends and family, and an inspiration to those who follow. Each year, as I speak to the graduates, I realize that the problem with graduations is that they only happen at the end of the levels of formal schooling. The truth is, that our most significant graduations happen throughout our lives. Those graduations often go unheralded, even by ourselves.

All our lives we graduate. We pass from one stage of experience, insight and knowledge to a higher one. We change gradually. Our life is not just about what we do, but about who we become, regardless of, or because of, our job, position, vocation, commitments, relationships, strengths or weaknesses. It takes more than a diploma to map out the journey that our life takes as our soul seeks to fulfill God's purpose in us. It takes more than academic preparation to consecrate ourselves to that purpose. It takes more than a Degree to live the kind of hope that frees us to know how to live in the world without being imprisoned by it. Who benefits from the life we live? How do we live out our lives in community with others while confronting, questioning, supporting, or defending the environment in which the human person is formed? When was the last time we graduated?

I know that what I had planned for my life at my formal graduations, any of them, looks nothing like the life I lead today. Maybe yours doesn't either. Perhaps your most significant graduations have gone unnoticed, even by you. Maybe it's time to graduate again to the next higher level of who you are becoming. Maybe it's time for a graduation speech. I just happen to have one that I gave at a graduation that I would like to share with you as you graduate to your next level.

Dear graduates, I have come to tell you, each of you, that you have been anointed by God to make a difference in this world, a difference that only you can make. He has anointed you with a mission He has not given to anyone else. And, with His anointing, you have received from God all the grace and courage you need to fulfill in you, His promise of greatness. I really don't know what it is that God has anointed you to do. Maybe you don't either. But He does. Ask Him. Pray. And while you wait for an answer, because God's time is not our time, let your light shine. Let your gifts and good works illuminate the journey you take. You won't know if you're on the right path if you're stumbling around in the dark. And then, one day, you will know. You'll feel it. You'll sense it. You'll discover just what it is that God has anointed you to do. Not only are you anointed, you will also be appointed. There will be others in your life who will give you the opportunities you need to fulfill your purpose in life. Listen to them. What they are saying might not sound like what you were planning to do with your life, but listen to them anyway. Do you hear God's voice? It could be tomorrow. It could be thirty years from now. Don't be afraid. Say "yes". Take that leap of faith. It won't be easy. There will be struggles. But if in those struggles, you are doing what God has anointed and others appointed you to do, then the light you shine, each in your own way, will illuminate the path the world will take. And you will know that the work you do, whatever it is, is God's. Go now, and be light and hope for the world. Congratulations!

~

Dismiss The Crowd

There is a passage from Walt Whitman's Leaves Of Grass that says: "A child goes forth each day and the first object that the child sees, that object he becomes, for a day, or part of a day, or for days stretching into years". For our children, what they see in our society is what they will become, for a day, or part of a day or days stretching into years. What is it that we want our children to become? It is not material poverty that causes violence and all kinds of self- destructive behavior in our society. It is spiritual poverty. It is a poverty of the soul that robs our children of their dreams and us of the hope of reclaiming them.

We can feed the hungry, clothe the naked, give drink to the thirsty, but how do you breathe oxygen into the soul? How do you give the gift of transcendent freedom to those who are beaten down by the intent of others to use power for greed or ambition for evil? We live in a very difficult time in which to keep children innocent and adults courageous. We are pulled in every direction by the demands of instant gratification. The crowd of voices that only seeks to destroy, even in the name of love, diverts us from our purpose. But wise love demands transformation rather than reinforcement. And God, in His wisdom, so loved the world that He sent His only Son, not to transform, but to be transformation.

How do we bring about that transformation? What is it we want our children to become, for a day, or part of a day or days stretching into years? Not just our children, but all children, even the ones nobody claims as their own. What will give life to the vision for our children of a world, rooted in love, where virtues are non-negotiable and character development a way of life? How do we have the audacity to think that there can be transformation in a world so mired in self-destruction? Where will we get the courage to hold up all our choices against this vision and act in a way that leads to its realization? There is only one answer. Dismiss the crowd.

Do what Jesus did when the skeptics said, "Who does He think He is, this son of a carpenter?" He dismissed them and did what He knew He could do. Do what Jesus did when the naysayers did not think it was possible to feed the multitude with a handful of food, make the blind see, raise the dead, turn water into wine, or walk on water. He dismissed them, and did what He knew; that with God, all things are possible. Do what Jesus did when others told Him that He was not going about His mission in the right way. He dismissed them and did what His Father asked of Him. He kept His eyes on the prize. He even dismissed his Apostles when they tried to dissuade Him. He dismissed Peter when he lost sight of the vision and told him, "Get thee behind me, Satan". And in the garden, on the eve of His death, when things got really tough, not wanting to be persuaded against fulfilling His purpose, He dismissed them all and said "Sit down. I'm going to pray."

We were not in the desert with Jesus, but He is always in the desert with us. Maybe it is time for us to dismiss the crowd, to dismiss all the negative voices in our society. Dismiss all that seeks to destroy our spirit. Dismiss all that is holding us back from fulfilling our purpose as people of faith. It is time to dismiss the crowd and pray for the strength, courage and wisdom it will take to overcome those who would sabotage our efforts to ensure that the children, all God's children, go forth each day into a world of hope.

~

Are We There Yet?

No matter how old we are, how many trips we take, or whom we go with, there is a universal question that seems to accompany every journey: "Are we there yet?" I was reminded of this phenomenon while taking two of my grandchildren to visit a friend. We were only into the third mile of a sixty-mile trip when I heard the first "Are we there yet?" Actually, with detours and construction traffic I was beginning to think we would never be there. I remembered how I would try to distract my children on long trips when they were young. I attempted to shift their focus from the journey by talking about what we would do when we finally arrived. I thought it was a good plan at the time. In thinking about it now, I think I only made the trip more unbearable by heightening their eagerness to get there. Now, here I was with my grandchildren. I felt like I had just been given a "do over" from God. So I approached their question in a different light.

I told my grandchildren we weren't there yet and I had no idea when we would get there. I told them to look around at where we are now. What do they see that could make our trip longer or shorter, more fun or scary? What could keep us going or keep us from getting there? What would we do if we couldn't get there from here? The trip soon became a vision quest and we the adventurers of a great mission. We made it! Even the dinosaur that ate I-40 couldn't stop us. We kept our focus on our final destination. Although there were many dangers, obstacles and challenges, we were going to fearlessly and firmly proceed. Nothing was going to stop us from getting there, eventually.

In that experience I discovered two spiritually productive truths: Children haven't changed, childhood has. And, obedience to God requires courage.

As parents, as educators, as anyone charged with the responsibility for children today, we need courage to stand in the face of a materialistic society with a self-serving code of conduct and speak out on behalf of the children, no matter how dangerous it is to do so. Are we there yet? Can we do that with the courage of our convictions? If not, what's the obstacle? We need the kind of courage only God can give to be on this mission He has given us to parent, to teach, and to protect the children. Are we there yet? Are we even on the way? Have we taken stock of the pitfalls around us that can keep us from shepherding our children through the valley of darkness that our society often becomes for them? Have we allowed them to be lured into the midst of wolves?

In times of ease we become secure in the established order, however imperfect, and we begin to take everything for granted, even our children, even God. What has crept into childhood today was never meant to be there. They experience a culture that glorifies adult behavior by children   Yet, we accept it by not noticing the music they listen to, the clothes they wear, the shows they watch, the language they speak or the games they play. And if we do notice it, we assume it is childhood today and we say nothing. We are convinced that we are on the right road because the road is so crowded. What is our destination for our children? What is distracting us from helping them get there? Are we headed in the right direction? Who is going our way?

When we are on the journey that God has mapped out for us, and for our children, we won't have to ask if we are there yet, we'll know. The traffic might get lighter but the travelers get more courageous. Let us fearlessly and firmly proceed as we make the journey of childhood a vision quest for our children that will lead them to their final destination, no matter how long it takes to get there.

~

Footprints

There is a saying that some people come into our lives and quietly go. Others stay for a while and leave footprints on our hearts and we are never the same. I consider the footprints left on my heart as gifts. I would like to share some of my gifts with you.

Several years ago while waiting for an elevator at the Crescent Center, I struck up a conversation with a friendly man delivering a pair of freshly shined shoes to one of the offices. As I got off the elevator, he called after me, "Stop by my Shoe Shine stand if you're ever on the Lower Level". It was one of those days when I felt like the lower level of a building. The man's cheerfulness seemed so contagious that on my way out, I felt the need to stop by his stand. I learned that his name was Eddie. He grew up poor, in Memphis but worked hard and was on the way up in life. He moved to Chicago, got a great job, earned great money and had a great life. All that changed one night when he was robbed, savagely beaten and left for dead. After a long hospitalization, and a slow recovery, Eddie returned to Memphis so that his elderly father could take care of him. But he was never the same. Physically, he struggled to walk, experienced a great deal of pain and always wore a cap to cover the large indentation in his skull. Spiritually, he found God in his suffering and in his life. Once again he was on the way up. He had his own business now and still worked hard. He continually thanked God for the gift of life. He gave me a favorite book of prayers. I gave him an angel pin to wear on his cap. When at the Crescent Center, I'd stop by his stand. He was always ready with a smile and a sermonette. Both always lifted my spirits and made me appreciate the gift of my own life. It seemed his sole purpose was just to glorify God, and pass it on. Thanks, Eddie, for the gift of seeing God in living. It's a great gift.

Adriana was barely five when I first saw her, and not much more than six when I saw her last. She, her mother and her sister came to this country so that Adriana could receive treatment for her advancing cancer. Her sister was a student where I was Principal. Although Adriana was not able to attend school because of her illness, she would visit often. In spite of her painful treatments, she always had a smile and a way of leaving happiness wherever she went. Adriana's conditioned worsened and she was confined to bed. She was dying. When I visited her, she would draw pictures of hearts and stars and flowers for me. I would bring her pictures of angels and Jesus with the children and tell her that was what heaven looked like. The pictures compensated for my limited Spanish and her limited English. On my last visit there were no pictures from her, just a faint smile. So I sat by her bed, held her hand and prayed. When it was time for me to leave, she squeezed my hand and said, "I love you". I kissed her good-by and asked her to tell Jesus I said "Hi". I still have her drawings and her footprints on my heart. Thanks, Adriana, for the gift of seeing God in dying. It's a great gift.

Grandparents are noted for the things they teach their grandchildren. When I was a little girl, my grandfather taught me how to draw horns, beards and mustaches on people whose pictures were in the newspaper. With a twinkle in his eye, he told me it was always better to do this before anyone else read the paper. It would make it more interesting. We'd sit on the floor and get to work. I didn't think it really made anyone as happy as he thought it would because the ink always covered up the words on the other side of the page. But he'd laugh and we'd do it anyway. He'd laugh a lot. When I was eight my grandfather became very ill. One morning we got a call that he had taken a turn for the worse. The family gathered around his bed; his wife, ten children, in-laws and hoards of grandchildren. My aunt, Lillian, a Religious Sister, thought it would be a good idea to sprinkle my grandfather with holy water after we said the Rosary. She very ceremoniously waved the bottle in the direction of my grandfather. As she did, the top flew off and the entire contents of the bottle landed in my grandfather's face. He woke up, wiped his face, and with a fading twinkle in his eyes said, "You don't have to drown me, Lilly, I'm going as fast as I can". Everyone laughed. Thanks, Big Grandpop, for the gift of seeing God in laughter. It's a great gift.

Share the footprints left on your heart with others. Better still; leave your footprints of your own.

~

EPILOGUE

Life is not ended; merely changed. I believe that the best is yet to come. Take the journey and travel by The Light, reflected.

ABOUT THE AUTHOR

Dr. Mary Crowley McDonald is the Secretary of Education and Superintendent for the Catholic Diocese of Memphis. She was born and raised in Philadelphia and currently resides in Germantown, Tennessee with her husband, Joe. She has been involved in education since 1966 when she started teaching at St. Maria Goretti High School in Philadelphia. During her career, she taught at the elementary, high school and university levels. She served as a school Principal for fifteen years, and Superintendent of Schools since 1998.

Dr. McDonald earned her Bachelors degree from Immaculata College in Immaculata, Pennsylvania, her Masters degree from the University of St. Thomas in St. Paul Minnesota and her Doctorate from the University of Memphis in Memphis, Tennessee.

Dr. McDonald is a graduate of Leadership Memphis and serves on the Boards of Facing History and Ourselves, The Rotary Club of Memphis, and the Gateway Technology Educational Advisory Board. She is a member of the National Council for Community and Justice, The Equestrian Order of the Holy Sepulcher, Christian Brothers University President's Circle and as a Regional Representative for the National Catholic educational Association.

Dr. McDonald writes a regular column for the West Tennessee Catholic newspaper and is a featured writer in several other local and national newspapers and journals. She was named to Who's Who in American Education, is a recipient of the University of Notre Dame's Exemplar Award for outstanding contributions to the field of education and was the 2001 recipient of the Amethyst Award from Immaculata College. In 1999 she was named one of 50 Women Who Make A Difference in the Mid-South by Mid-South Women's Magazine. The National Conference for Community and Justice (NCCJ) named dr. McDonald as the recipient of their 2002 Humanitarian of the Year Award. She and her husband, Joe, have two adult children and six grandchildren.

A Light Reflected

The journey of a soul is driven by the search for the answers to three questions.

How do I overcome death? Not just physical death, but the small ways in which we die from loneliness, despair, the changes in our lives and the loss of our self-worth.

Does my life have meaning? Why I am here? Will the world, even one small piece of it, be a better place because of me?

Who walks with me on this journey? Where are the soul mates? How are we connected, one to the other?

A Light Reflected is a collection of lessons learned and taught. We are all teachers. We are all students. We learn from one another. We see into the life of things when we sense the interconnectedness of what happens as we journey through life. It is the light by which we travel that makes all the difference as to where we go, and how we get there. That light is reflected in the choices we make, the life we lead, what we teach and from whom we learn.

Dr. Mary Crowley McDonald was born and raised in Philadelphia, Pennsylvania. She is a wife, mother, grandmother, author, public speaker and educator. Since 1998 she has been the Superintendent of Catholic School for the Diocese of Memphis. Her career also includes being a classroom teacher, a graduate school instructor, and a school principal. Her writings and lectures have inspired people throughout the country. She is the recipient of numerous awards and citations for her work, including the National Conference for Community and Justice 2002 Humanitarian of the year Award and The University of Notre Dame's Exemplar Award for Outstanding Contributions to the Field of Education. In this book, she brings the compassion, insight and wisdom needed to mold our affection for a life well led.